W9-CAI-114

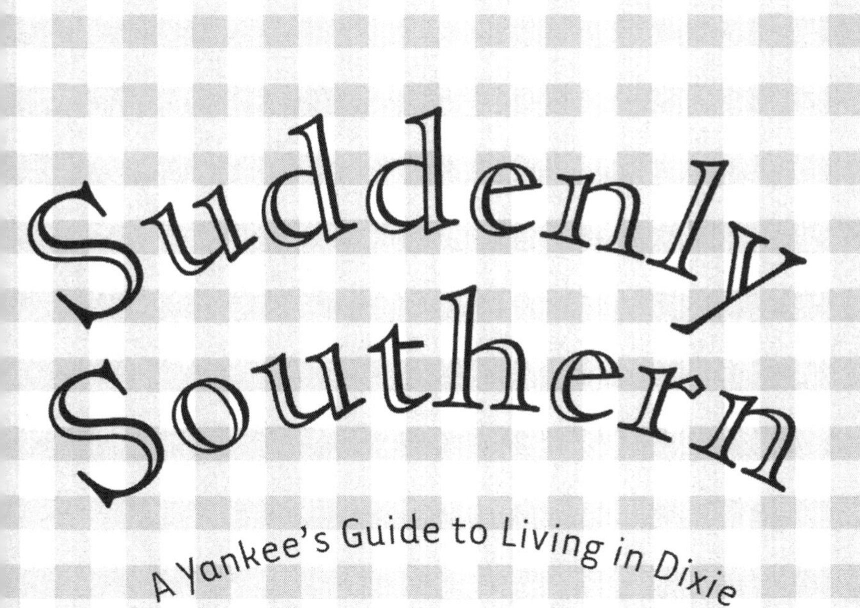


Maureen Duffin-Ward

Illustrations by Gary Hallgren

A Fireside Book
Published by Simon & Schuster
New York London Toronto Sydney

FIRESIDE
Rockefeller Center
1230 Avenue of the Americas
New York, NY 10020

Copyright © 2004 by Maureen Duffin-Ward
All rights reserved,
including the right of reproduction
in whole or in part in any form.

FIRESIDE and colophon are registered trademarks of Simon & Schuster, Inc.

For information regarding special discounts for bulk purchases,
please contact Simon & Schuster Special Sales at
1-800-456-6798 or business@simonandschuster.com

Designed by Diane Hobbing of Snap-Haus Graphics

Manufactured in the United States of America
10 9 8 7 6 5 4 3 2 1

Library of Congress Cataloging-in-Publication Data
Duffin-Ward, Maureen.
Suddenly southern : a Yankee's guide to living in Dixie / Maureen-Duffin Ward; illustrations by Gary Hallgren.
p. cm.
"A Touchstone Book."
1. Southern States—Social life and customs. 2. Southern States—Handbooks, manuals, etc. I. Title.
F209.D84 2004
975—dc22 2004048234

ISBN 978-0-7432-5495-3

*To my husband,*
*Michael Ward,*
*who was so worth the wait.*
*And so worth the move.*

# *Contents*

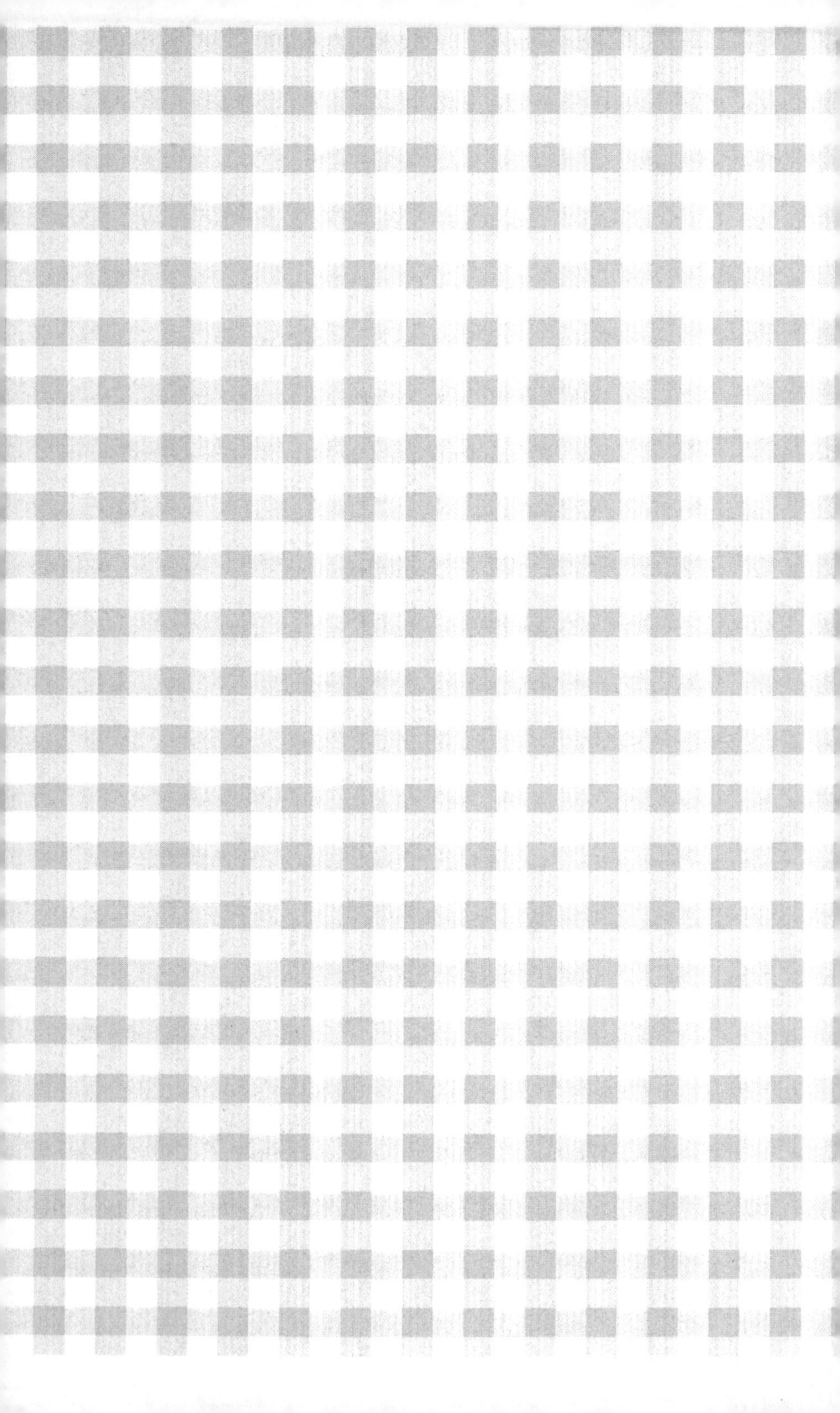

CHAPTER 1

★ ★ ★ ★ ★ ★ ★ ★ ★

# A Moving Target, or Toto, I Have a Feeling We're Not in Philly Anymore

***When your husband says,*** "Honey, ever been South?," be afraid—be very afraid. According to my grief counselor—I'm sorry, I mean relocation coach—the average person takes one year to adjust to a move. I guess that makes me below average. On my one-year anniversary in Raleigh, North Carolina, I:

- Could only sleep facing north.
- Still got told twice a week, "You sound like the Nanny!"
- Still flew to Philly for my haircuts.
- Got my local news by typing www.phillynews.com into the computer.
- Had called the police on my mailman. How was I to know the mailman drove a burnt-orange Chevrolet? All I knew was that there was a suspicious car parked outside the house and a man was rifling through the mailbox. That's a federal crime, right?

What brought me to Raleigh in the first place? Got a minute? We had been married about a year when Mr. Promotion shared the great news.

"They want me to run the NBC station in Raleigh, North Carolina."

"You tawkin' to me?"

For a born and bred Philly girl, that's like hearing "We're moving to Guam." Philly natives don't do moves. Our idea of relocation is making our way to the suburbs. And if all of your dreams come true, you get to buy a beach house "down the shore." Sure, the bold and the beautiful try to make it in New York. But the rest of us stay put. We don't know nothin' about no North Carolina.

My life was flashing before me. How could I leave my nephews? My nieces? My mother? My father? My sister? My brothers? My girlfriends! My career? My house? My routine? My life? My God!

But I knew if I said no, we'd be on the couch in six years, and my husband would be telling the good doctor how I ruined his life. I knew what I had to do.

"Sorry, no way."

And so the peace talks began. Michael pined for Pinehurst and golfing his way to the top. And I kind of liked the idea of getting out of all the baby and bridal showers I'd been attending. But missing my mom's Thanksgivings? Talk about misgivings. So this was going to be the catch that came with my catch: Fall in love, get married, and trade away the home and life I knew and loved.

Next thing you know we were going. And we are not alone. According to the census, about 40 million people move every year. And 40 percent of the people who move to a different region move to the South. The Yankee migration of the last twenty years won't just continue; experts say it will grow.

This book is for the hundreds of thousands of Yankee transplants who have moved south and haven't hit their stride yet. It will serve as a "been there, done that" for the reformed Yankees and "honorary Southerners" once removed. And it should provide plenty of mileage for the natives who think the damn Yankees should just take I-95 North.

My husband dragged me down here kicking and screaming, but I survived. And you will, too. Especially if you're open to a few survival tips:

| ***What to Pack*** | ***What Not to Pack*** |
|---|---|
| Your cocktail shaker | Your accent |
| Your art museum | Your sarcasm |
| A deep-fat fryer | Your *Zagat's America's Top Restaurants* |
| Case of Blue Ribbon | Case of the blues |
| A generator | Your opera glasses |
| Your hometown phone books | Your hometown cookbooks |
| A bread machine | Your rapid routine |
| Your pink flamingos | Your colorful Christmas lights and outdoor Santas (white lights only) |
| Gear for heavy rains | Snow gear and snow chains (expertise considered "showy") |
| Your daytime slippers | Your all-night dancing shoes |

**You Are Here**

According to Southerners, Yankees are never in "the real South." Geography be damned, everybody knows that Florida is not the real South; it's a suburb of NYC. But when you get to North Carolina, you'll hear, "Raleigh isn't the real South anymore, you have to go to Savannah or Tennessee." You get to Nashville and they say, "Oh, this isn't the real South; it's all New Yorkers now. You have to go to Alabama." Southerners just keep sending Yankees farther south to experience the "real thing." I think this is the Southern genteel way of saying "Go to hell."

Okay, open your eyes; you're home!!!

## *Different Strokes for Different Folks*

You thought New York's elite co-op boards had a hard time keeping out the riffraff. How about these Southern developments with houses going for $1 million, $2 million, did I hear $3 million and a Ferrari? I was able to get my hands on one of the "moving on up" applications. A couple of million and you're in.

## *Plantations R Us Application*

(If you and your wife have a combined handicap of more than 12, please accept our condolences, and y'all come back and see us real soon.)

### Part I

1. I am relocating from the North because
   a. I am a Ph.D. who discovered the cure for cancer, and Research Triangle Park says I'd make a nice junior-level applicant.
   b. My husband was transferred, and I'm a born follower.
   c. I'm a hurricane chaser.

2. With my net worth as of today, I could
   a. Pay off the fiscal deficit for the United States.
   b. Join any Southern country club and secure a seat on the board.
   c. Just about swing a dozen Krispy Kremes.

3. In your estimation, which of these egregious crimes should result in the death penalty:
   a. Hanging a clothesline
   b. Having a nonconforming mailbox or choosing a fence or bird feeder without approval from the architectural board
   c. None of the above

### Part II

4. The family most resembling yours is
   a. Aunt Bee and the gang from *The Andy Griffith Show*
   b. The Wilkes of Twelve Oaks
   c. *The Sopranos*

5. You are most likely to vote yes on the following referendums:
   a. Changing the name of the airport to Mayberry International
   b. A commemorative stamp for the United Daughters of the Confederacy
   c. Free Mumia!

**To the Applicant: If you answered c to more than one of the above questions, please fill out the attached form, "Request for a Pardon from the Governor," put your keys in the basket, and wait for the police escort up I-95 North.**

**Part III**

The Formal Interview. (Please come accompanied by a Southern sponsor.)

## *Creating Your Southern House*

The bigger, the better!!! Let's face it, we all bragged to our Yankee friends about the cost of living down here. And yeah, we pretty much crowed we could buy a mansion the size of Tara for what they're paying for their L-shape studio in New York. Now it's time to put up or shut up. Take advantage of low interest rates and get yourself in deep hock. Consider new construction.

First a word about our Southern builders. Make that two words: career criminals. They're just like the big bad builders in the rest of the country, so don't let their warm Southern accent, their "yes, sirs" and "no, ma'ams," and their piety lull you into a false sense of security. Southern builders know very little about keeping a deadline, but they know quite a bit about God-fearing values and aren't afraid to use them in marketing. Christians will he happy to know there are Christian builders, Christian heating and air-conditioning workers, and Christian plumbers. (Atheists will be happy to know there's do-it-yourself.)

**Yankee Do! Get a good exterminator, and put him on speed dial. The bugs are as big as cats down here.**

KNOW YOUR BUGS
ACTUAL SIZE
BY THEIR MUGS
PALMETTO BUG
FIRE ANT
JUNE BUG
I LUV U
JULY BUG
M-80
DRAGONFLY
BOWL WEEVIL
KILLER BEE
HORSE FLY
MOSQUITO
CUPBOARD MOTH
CEREAL
YELLOW CATERPILLAR
GNATS

### *Furnishing Your First Porch*

- Antique wicker settee and matching chair—Southerners pass these down through the generations (or so they claim; wild how wicker holds up for two hundred years here)
- A swing
- Yellow or green pillows
- Hanging fuchsia plant (white wicker preferred, macramé second choice)
- Potted plants—simple, not showy

Your new house may take some getting used to. Sure, you took out a two-hundred-year mortgage on it, and it's grander than anything you ever dreamed you would own, but then you get inside. Apparently, these stately manors are designed mostly for the neighbors. The entire house is on the outside (including furniture). Southerners spend at least ten months a year on their porch. Or is that verandah? Here's what it's not: the deck. If you want to fit in down here, hanging outdoors means right out where everyone can see what you're doing. Down in front! Southerners are porch people, not deck dwellers. Sitting (or swinging) on the

porch means "we're accepting visitors," so Southerners always keep a book within arm's reach. The book is "read" when an undesirable is in waving distance. Reading the book is the refined way of telling the prospective caller (a Yankee newcomer, for instance), "Alas, we'll pass."

Meanwhile, you walk up to your plantation, and you walk into, well, Plantation Junior. The living room and the dining room are a lot like the dollhouse you had as a child: miniature. You will never fit all of your dining room furniture, unless you're fortunate like me; I didn't have any. The "parlor" is for seeing, not sitting. And don't even think about putting the furniture that doesn't fit upstairs down in the basement. There is no basement. We live in perpetual fear of water damage down here. The thinking is: If I don't have a basement, I won't have a basement flood. Hah!

Once you've decided on location, location, location, it's decoration, decoration, decoration. If you really want to blend in, you'll hire your own interior designer so your décor will be up to code. If you are house-poor—and sure, poor, poor, too—you will have to fake it. Lucky for you, there's *Southern Living.*

If the whole South were a hotel, the Bible would be in the left drawer next to the bed and *Southern Living* would be in the right drawer. Any Yankee can get a copy (I think the subscription fee might be a buck or two higher for Yankees), but, hey, it's a must if you want a real Southern house.

## Southern Comforts, or Must-Haves for Your Southern House

- **Curtains!**

You must cover everything. A one-inch peephole? Needs a window treatment. The garage portal? Gingham. For your more important windows, it's all about drama. If it wouldn't look out of place in the Queen of England's library, it won't look out of place here. The sun is something we hide from in the South. Air conditioning wasn't invented when Great-Grandmother decorated her house, and to do something different would be, well, just disrespecting her.

- **Grandma's Relics**

Southerners pay tribute to Grandma by displaying as many of her old relics as possible. Family heirlooms are key to proving genuine heritage. Grandma's genteel china saucers arranged in a mobile work well as a chandelier, and they keep the conversation focused on family.

**Yankee Do! Hit a flea market and pick up some old junk. It's "Grandmother's" from that point forward.**

- **Pastels**

Now it's time to add color. Yellows, greens, reds, and blues—what Southerners call "their colors." (You may know them as the primary colors.)

- **Portraits**

Portraiture is alive and well in the South, and you'll want a $10,000 likeness for each member of the family. A bridal portrait is necessary front and center no matter how many years ago he carried you over the threshold.

**Unanswered Questions:** If you decorate your house with fifty ideas under $50 from *Southern Living,* how many clay pots will you have?

## *Your Library*

At this point, you should be ready to go to the local or online bookstore and order 721 coffee table books on the Civil War. You must put at least twelve in each room of the house. If you really want to win friends and influence people, have the books opened to battles the Southerners won. Tomes of General Lee get the best views. Abraham Lincoln goes in the downstairs john. Jefferson Davis, the parlor. The Battle of Gettysburg—the garage. Here's a handy guide for a larger house. (Remember, less room doesn't mean fewer books!)

| | |
|---|---|
| Parlor: | • *Lee*<br>• *The United States at War: The Civil War: All You Want to Know*<br>• *Jefferson Davis Biography* |
| Dining Room: | • *The Battle of Fredericksburg* |
| Family Room: | • *The Library of Congress Civil War Desk Reference*<br>• *R. E. Lee: A Biography*<br>• *Virginia's General: Robert E. Lee and the Civil War* |
| Master Bedroom: | • *Stonewall Jackson: The Man, The Soldier, The Legend*<br>• *A Confederate's Memoirs of the Civil War* |
| Bathroom #1: | • *Lincoln at Gettysburg: The Words That Remade America* |
| Kitchen: | • *The Civil War Cookbook* |
| Office: | • *Encyclopedia of the Confederacy* (4-volume set) |
| Kid's Bedroom: | • *The War Within: A Novel of the Civil War* |
| Guest Bedroom: | • *Southern Quilts: Surviving Relics of the Civil War* |
| Guest Bathroom: | • *Gettysburg, Day Three* |
| Laundry Room: | • *Where I'm Bound: A Civil War Novel* |
| Garage: | • *The Gettysburg Campaign: A Study in Command* |

## *Your Vacation House*

I don't mean to pressure you right away (one new house is enough of a challenge), but it won't be long before you realize that "everybody" has a place to escape the summer heat.

### Naming Your Southern Beach House

Rentals are fine, but ownership is finer. Southerners with money need you to know they don't take themselves too seriously. In the South, it's less about new money versus old money and more about real Southerners versus "honorary Southerners." Naming the beach house is the perfect opportunity to prove (1) you're born and bred; (2) your renting days are behind you; (3) you can never be too rich or too cutesy. It's also an ideal way to pledge your allegiance to your college football team.

Okay, the first test is behind you. You've picked a house(s). You've made it a home. It's official. You live in the South. Now it's time to unpack and meet the neighbors.

**Yankee Don't! Refrain from using sarcastic, in-your-face names.**

Chapter 2

# Close Encounters of the Southern Kind, or Don't You Be My Neighbor

***Remember that sitcom,*** *3rd Rock from the Sun,* where aliens from another planet think the Earthlings are the ones who are strange? It's like that here. Southerners are convinced the Yankees are crazy, and Yankees believe the Southerners are from out of this world. I'm still not sure who's right. But I do know this: If you want to understand the inhabitants of your new, exciting universe, you'll need this handy field guide.

## The Three Types of Southern Men

### #1 Daddy

**Distinguishing Physical Trait:** White hair and blue eyes

**High School Trademark:** Voted most likely to play Santa

**Defined Today by:** His handicap

**Favorite Pastime:** The club

**Book on His Nightstand:** *Peak Performance Golf* by Patrick Cohn

**CD in the Car:** *Heart Stoppers and Hail Marys: 100 of the Greatest College Football Finishes* by Ted Mandell

**Personal Hero:** Strom Thurmond (R.I.P.)

**Bumper Sticker:** Rush is Right

### #2 Politico

**Distinguishing Physical Trait:** Rosacea

**High School Trademark:** Voted most likely to run for office

**Defined Today by:** State fair appearances

**Favorite Pastime:** Backroom deals and smoking stogies

**Book on His Nightstand:** *Master of the Senate: The Years of Lyndon Johnson* by Robert A. Caro

**CD in the Car:** Books on Tape: *The Seven Habits of Highly Effective People* by Stephen R. Covey

**Personal Hero:** His father

**Bumper Sticker:** Give 'em Helms

### #3 Redneck

**Distinguishing Physical Trait:** Body art

**High School Trademark:** Shop class's most likely to succeed

**Defined Today by:** Pickup with two-gun rack

**Favorite Pastime:** The Dew Drop Inn

**Book on His Nightstand:** 101 Dumb Blonde Jokes (Internet download) and *The Mullet: Hairstyle of the Gods* by Mark Larson, Barney Hoskyns, and Maria Burgaleta Larson

**CB in the Car:** Channel 9 ("Breaker, Breaker, Red Hen, Come on, Come on")

**Personal Hero:** Dale Earnhardt

**Bumper Sticker:** Go ahead and honk. I'm reloading.

✯ ✯ ✯ ✯ ✯ ✯ ✯ ✯ ✯

## *Quiz #1 Famous Southern Men (match column A with column B)*

| Column A | Column B |
| --- | --- |
| 1. Michael Jordan | A. One of the better imports from New York |
| 2. Jimmy Carter | B. Knows how to please the majority |
| 3. Martin Sheen | C. Knows how to displease the majority |
| 4. George Clooney | D. Your vote counts! But not as much as his. |
| 5. Bill Clinton | E. Throws presidential picnics. Prefers flies to black ties. |
| 6. Muhammad Ali | F. Gets top $ for his legal briefs. |
| 7. Trent Lott | G. His prayers for the White House may be answered. |
| 8. Clarence Thomas | H. *He's not Southern!* |
| 9. Billy Graham | I. The greatest of all time |
| 10. John Grisham | J. Leading man |

**Answer Key: AEHBJICDGF**

If you got less than five right, maybe you should register as an alien.
If you got five to seven right, you're a little bit country, a little bit rock 'n' roll.
If you got eight to ten right, you're good. You're damn good.

## The Three Types of Southern Women

### #1 Southern Belle (a.k.a. Daddy's Little Girl or the Deb)

**Distinguishing Physical Trait:** Blond hair
**High School Trademark:** Cheerleading squad/homecoming queen
**Defined Today by:** Her sorority
**Favorite Pastime:** Junior League
**Book on Her Nightstand:** *Divine Secrets of the Ya-Ya Sisterhood* by Rebecca Wells
**CD in the Car:** *Home* by Dixie Chicks (She can forgive their Bush bashing even though Daddy can't.)
**Personal Hero:** Daddy
**China Pattern:** Spode

### #2 Daughters of the Confederacy

**Distinguishing Physical Trait:** Nose in the air
**High School Trademark:** Church choir
**Defined Today by:** Visits to the graveyard
**Favorite Pastime:** Battlefield visits during the week, services on Sunday
**Book on Her Nightstand:** The Holy Bible
**CD in the Car:** *Amazing Grace: His Greatest Sacred Performances* by Elvis Presley
**Personal Hero:** Daddy
**China pattern:** Wedgewood

## #3 Mrs. Redneck

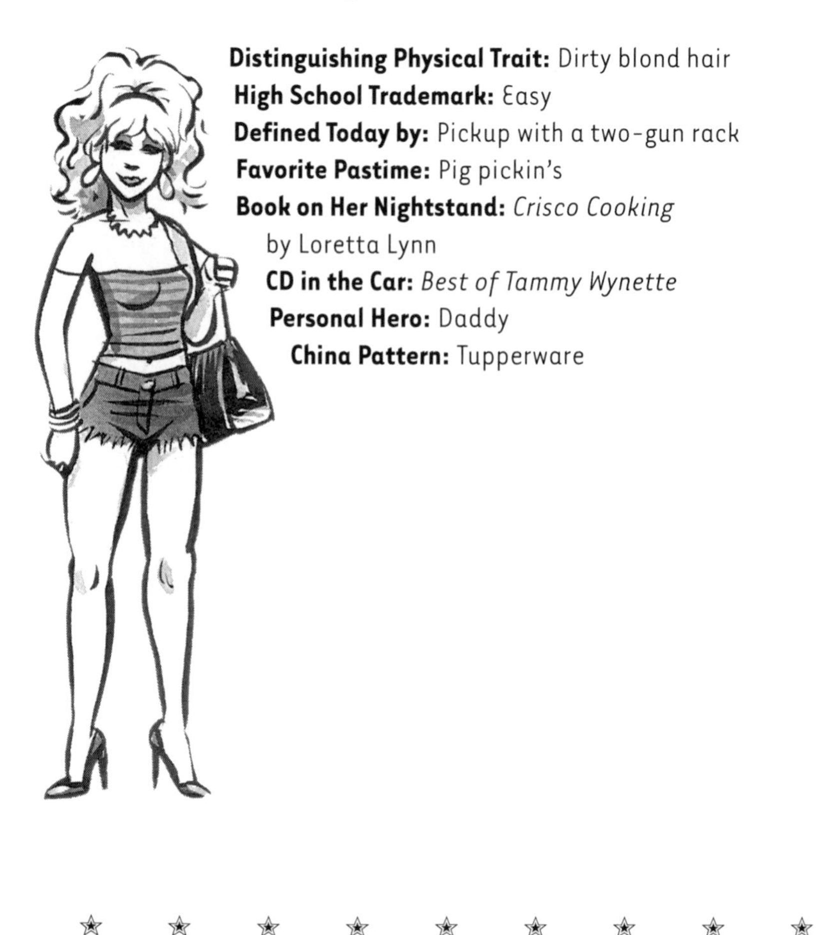

**Distinguishing Physical Trait:** Dirty blond hair
**High School Trademark:** Easy
**Defined Today by:** Pickup with a two-gun rack
**Favorite Pastime:** Pig pickin's
**Book on Her Nightstand:** *Crisco Cooking* by Loretta Lynn
**CD in the Car:** *Best of Tammy Wynette*
**Personal Hero:** Daddy
**China Pattern:** Tupperware

★ ★ ★ ★ ★ ★ ★ ★ ★

## *Belles Are Born, Not Made*

Yankee moms who deliver their baby girls in the South believe themselves suddenly elevated to Southern gentry. They insist they have a legitimate Southern belle in the family. But it takes more than longitude and latitude to deliver just the right attitude. Is she or isn't she?

**How You Know If You Gave Birth to a Baby Belle**

- She's born with a silver spoon in her mouth and cries when it's not her pattern.
- She wears a straw hat instead of a baby bonnet.
- She tells the obstetrician how smart he is.
- When the doctor whacks her in the delivery room, she tells her daddy.
- Her bottle is full of buttermilk.
- Her hospital ID has charms on it.
- Her diapers are 300 count.
- Her stroller has curtains on it.
- She's born with frosted blond hair.
- She cries with a Southern drawl.
- She wears a cover-up in the birth canal.
- She'll only be burped in the ladies' room.
- She thinks teething rings are tacky.
- She's born with a magnolia pink manicure and pedicure.
- She writes her own birth announcement.

## *Quiz #2 Famous Southern Women (match column A with column B)*

| ***Column A*** | ***Column B*** |
|---|---|
| 1. Julia Roberts | A. She's out of this world. |
| 2. Oprah | B. The camera(man) loves her. |
| 3. Sally Field in *Norma Rae* | C. She put us on the map. |
| 4. Elizabeth Dole | D. This southern blonde is legal. |
| 5. Kim Basinger | E. World's worst fake Southern accent |
| 6. Barbra Streisand | F. Plays Monopoly with Georgia |
| 7. Eudora Welty | G. Married Southern. |
| 8. Shirley MacLaine | H. *She's not Southern!* |
| 9. Reese Witherspoon | I. Monica was the girl next door. |
| 10. Hillary Clinton | J. "All serious daring starts from within." |

**Answer Key: BCEIFHJADG**

If you got less than five right, you need to renew your subscription to *People.*
If you got five to seven right, you're a lady's lady.
If you got eight to ten right, you're walk of fame material.

## *What's in a Name?*

### What's-his-name and What's-her-name

Shelby, Kingston, Taylor? Meet Manny, Moe, and Jack. The Pep Boys must be Yankees. No self-respecting Southern gent would sport such a common name. A surname anywhere else in the country is a first name here, and many of them seem to have been inspired by tobacco inheritances. Reynolds, Winston, and Chesterfield are a few of the top brands, er, names. It's also completely acceptable, encouraged

### Top Ten Baby Names for Girls

| Southern | Yankee |
|---|---|
| Adna | Kayla |
| Agnes | Alex |
| Burmah | Brianna |
| Clarice | Denise |
| Clementine | Cheryl |
| Dessie | Jessie |
| Merleen | Irene |
| Peggy Sue | Margaret Ann (Maggie) |
| Stancy | Nancy |
| Tammy Lynn | Tina |

### Top Ten Baby Names for Boys

| Southern | Yankee |
|---|---|
| Beauregard | Bernie |
| Bubba | Bro' |
| Billy Bob | Deuce |
| Danforth | Dude |
| Farnsworth | Frank |
| Hunter | Harry |
| Jeb | Gino |
| Junior | Jerry |
| Luther Ray | Dr. J. |
| Rutherford | Rocky |

even, to name children after dead college football coaches. Good ole boys cursed with more typical handles like Charles or William do the best they can to command authority. Charlie might be a good name for tuna, but not for a man with dignity. Call him by his formal name, or don't call him at all. Chuck and Bill need not apply. Unless, of course, he's presidential material, where being approachable is what it's all about. Bubba in '08.

To keep things interesting, Southern belles also sport men's names. Daddy's little girl may act like Miss Priss, but her name is all man. Hunter, Stuart, and Reed wear dresses. If they go with a girly-girl name, unique spellings are a plus. And middle names are a must.

Meet Rebekah Lynn, Kathryn Elizabeth, and Pattie Lee. The Billy Bobs and Bobby Sues live mostly in TV land and maybe a few in the rural areas. It's expected that Southern babies will grow into their names, so it's no surprise when Momma and Daddy look at their beautiful baby twins and say, "It's a miracle of life. Let's call him Clovis and her Beulah."

Southerners have easy-to-say last names: Todd, King, Bonds, Stone, Phillips, Davis. They didn't grow up with schoolteachers pronouncing their names incorrectly at roll call. So forgive them when they can barely stifle a laugh when they say, "Teach me how to pronounce your funny last name again!" Kakissis? Wolowiec? Martinez? *"Y'all not from around here, are ya?"*

### Married with Hyphen

It is said down here that Southern women have two first names and Yankee women have two last names. It's all about tradition down South, so getting married and not taking your husband's name—well, *it just ain't right.* Yankees with hyphens always hold up the line, whether they're trying to vote in an election or pick up their dry cleaning; the Southerner in charge usually has little patience for the novelty. "Yeah, but which one of these is your last name, ma'am?"

**Yankee Do! Leave your hyphen at the MasonHyphenDixon Line.**

★ ★ ★ ★ ★ ★ ★ ★ ★

## *That's Entertainment!*

### TV Guide (Southerners Only)

Forget "Must See TV" and MTV, Southerners just want their "Aunt Bee TV." Southerners need a TiVo that edits the programs, not just the commercials. As long as the advertising spokesperson has a *genuine* Southern accent, Southerners don't complain about the commercials. It's the Yankee shows that cause the stress. Southerners can't relate to the fast-talking, "racy" Yankee sitcoms and left-wing liberal dramas; they long for the good ole days of *The Andy Griffith Show.* If only there were a device that could Southernize programs.

**This Schedule Has Been Brought To You by Southern TiVo**

| | |
|---|---|
| NBC: | *Will and Gracious Me* |
| ABC: | *8 Simple Rules for Dating My Southern Daughter* |
| CBS: | *Survivor: Nashville* |
| Fox: | *Who Wants to Marry a Civil War Reenactor?* |
| HBO: | *Prevent Sex in the City* |
| HBO: | *Six Feet & Under* (a series about ACC and SEC students who aren't on a basketball scholarship) |
| Cable: | *All Opie, All the Time* |
| Bravo: | *Queer Eye for the Krispy Kreme Guy* |

## *Dixie's Digests, or Mags of Magnolia*

Southerners love to kick back and enjoy a good magazine. They prefer the hometown team to the "visitors," so anything with South or Southern in the title, subtitle, or masthead is likely to make the cut. Magazines that originate from the rest of the country are for, well, the rest of the country. Who needs *Sports Illustrated* when *Southern Living* covers ACC football the way it should be covered—with the focus on Southern teams?! And a recipe to boot. A typical magazine rack in a Southern den:

*Southern Living*
*Southern Accents*
*Southern Cultures*
*Veranda Magazine*
*Guns & Ammo*
*South Carolina Game & Fish*

**Yankee Don't! Never buy those perfectly awful tabloid magazines at the checkout counter in the supermarket—especially when a Daughter of the Confederacy is bearing witness. Join her as she moves her head slowly from side to side and say, "How vulgar."**

**Yankee Do! Order one as soon as you get home! (Unless you want to be the last to know that Elvis has impregnated Rosie O'Donnell.)**

## At Play with DNA (or Genes R Us)

### Let's give it up for the nutty professor. He decoded the DNA of a Northerner vs. a Southerner.

| Chromosome | Yankees | Southerners |
| --- | --- | --- |
| Pair 1 | All in all, I'd rather be in Philadelphia. | Not me, I prefer to live in the past. |
| Pair 2 | NFL | ACC or NASCAR |
| Pair 3 | Making it | Faking it |
| Pair 4 | Ability to laugh at themselves | We'll tell the jokes around here. |
| Pair 5 | Robs banks | Owns banks |
| Pair 6 | Me, Me, Me | My mama |
| Pair 7 | Sense of irony | Error, Error |
| Pair 8 | Mind your business! | Mind your manners! |
| Pair 9 | Interior design—is the fridge full? | Interior design: See *Southern Living.* |
| Pair 10 | Marries for money | Marries for Mummy (Mama) |
| Pair 11 | Protestant work ethic | Tomorrow is another day. |
| Pair 12 | I love the big city. | Raleigh is a big city; we have bagels. |

*(continued on next page)*

| Chromosome | Yankees | Southerners |
|---|---|---|
| Pair 13 | Speak my mind | Hold my tongue |
| Pair 14 | Competitive | Repetitive |
| Pair 15 | Woody Allen humor | Opie—now, he's funny. |
| Pair 16 | Tries everything | Fries everything |
| Pair 17 | Comes out of the closet at eighteen | Comes out as a deb at eighteen |
| Pair 18 | Drives a hard bargain | Drives a 4 x 4 |
| Pair 19 | Finishes your sentence for you | Finishes your pecan pie for you |
| Pair 20 | Big on reality | Big on morality |
| Pair 21 | Sunday is . . . HBO | Sunday is . . . Peace be with you, especially you with the covered dish. |
| Pair 22 | Honks the horn: Get out of the way. | Toots the horn: Have a nice day. |
| **X** | | Southerners are from Venus. |
| **Y** | Yankees are from Mars. | |

## *The Last Word on Southerners (and Their Little Pets, too)*

Southerners are both of proud pedigree and a breed apart. You can learn a lot about them from their pets. The Iams Company "It All Starts with a Name" survey found little variation in pet naming trends among age groups, but it discovered clear differences among regions. According to the research, Southerners are almost twice as likely as the rest of the country to name their puppy a silly name. And they also lead the nation in silly cat names. *Meow. Meow.* But let's leave Yum-Yum, Tuna Breath, Fatty Lump, and Pooty out of it.

### *You know your cat's a Southerner when . . .*

- Her favorite meal is Purina grits.
- She covers her mouth when she yawns.
- She wears a tiara.
- Her litter box is lined in lace.
- She thinks the dog is a slobbering idiot, bless his heart.
- She has her portrait made.
- She prefers her tuna fried.
- She belongs to a sorority.
- Her scratching tree was featured in *Southern Living.*

### *You know your dog's a Yankee when . . .*

- He knows how to pee his name in the snow.
- He gets in fights at Yappy Hour.
- He barks with a Brooklyn accent.
- He has Burberry chew toys.
- He prefers Bagels 'n Bits to Kibbles 'n Bits.
- He gets his toilet water from Starbucks.
- He dated Eddie on *Frasier.*
- He only eats Prada shoes.
- He asks for a better cage at the kennel: "Do you have something closer to the kitchen?"

★ ★ ★ ★ ★ ★ ★ ★ ★

## *Quiz #3 Are You Southern?*

**1. A mess of fish is**
- A. Part of the Passover meal
- B. Enough for both of us
- C. Dead catfish washed ashore
- D. All of the above

**2. What is cattywampus?**
- A. A direction
- B. A person who gossips
- C. A worm
- D. A cat in heat

**3. What is COWPIE?**
- A. Cow manure
- B. Country Or Western People In Earnest
- C. A chocolate marshmallow snack
- D. A cutie pie

**4. The first four words to the Southern national anthem are**
- A. "I pledge allegiance to"
- B. "In God we trust"
- C. "Gentlemen, start your engines"
- D. "Mine eyes have seen"

**5. Cheerwine is**
- A. A soda
- B. A pop
- C. A coke
- D. A red wine with fruit

**6. Why is fishing such a popular pastime for Southerners?**
- A. It's easier than bridge.
- B. It's a chance to outsmart your opponent.
- C. There's no fine for FUI (Fishing Under the Influence).
- D. It's in their nature.

*(continued on next page)*

7. **What will a Southern belle do when she doesn't get her way?**
   A. Pitch a hissie fit
   B. Throw a conniption
   C. Go to pieces
   D. All of the above

8. **Redeye Gravy is**
   A. An all-boy band
   B. Nickname for a hangover
   C. Served with breakfast
   D. A Willie Nelson song

9. **What did Margaret Mitchell originally name her famous heroine in *Gone With the Wind?***
   A. Scarlett O'Hara
   B. Pansy O'Hara
   C. Tara O'Hara
   D. Maureen O'Hara

10. **Who played Andy Griffith's son Opie?**
   A. Ronald Reagan
   B. Ron Howard
   C. Danny Bonaduce
   D. Greg Brady

**Answer Key: BAACCDDCBB**

If you got less than five right, you've never been south of New Jersey.
If you got five to eight right, you may live in the South, but not in the "Real South."
If you got nine to ten right, you're Southern born and Southern bred, and when you die you'll be Southern dead.

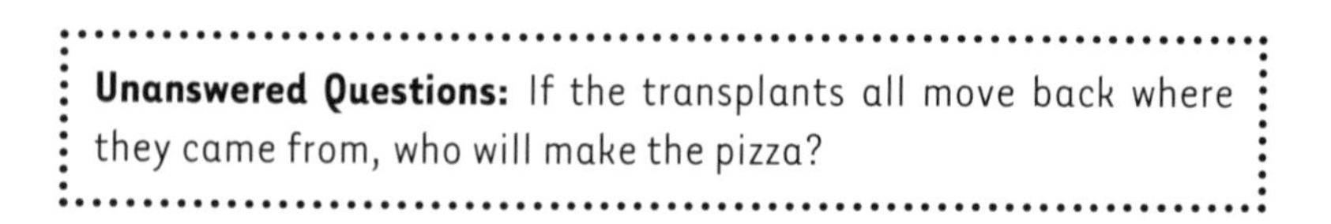
**Unanswered Questions:** If the transplants all move back where they came from, who will make the pizza?

## *Southern Horoscopes*

TAR HEEL

(MARCH 21–APRIL 20)

Once Tar Heels put their foot down, the rest is history. They tend to get stuck on things. The trick for those involved with Tar Heels is getting equal time during basketball season. They have a one-track mind, and they don't play well with others. The good news is they're extremely loyal.

KRISPY KREME

(APRIL 21–MAY 20)

North, South, East, or West, people can't get enough of Krispy Kremes. Men, women, and children will stand in line just to get to them. Not only are Krispy Kremes great fun, they do well in business, too.

PECAN PIE

(MAY 21–JUNE 21)

Some Pecan Pies are more nuts than others, and variety is the name of the game. Some are syrupy sweet, while others cut the sweetness by being downright tart.

(JUNE 22–JULY 22)
Fried Green Tomatoes tend to be dramatic by their very nature. While many are at home at the local farmer's market, plenty entertain delusions of grandeur. They see themselves on the big screen. Tart, crusty outside, mushy inside. Homey yet chic.

(JULY 23–AUGUST 22)
Southerners born under this sign are wildly popular, especially with their own. Sweet Teas are happiest when they are in the hands of someone they trust. When the discussions get heated, Sweet Teas know just how to cool things off.

(AUGUST 23–SEPTEMBER 22)
Strangers often have no idea of what to make of Pig Pickin's, but they're fun once you get to know them. They like to be the center of attention, even if it means having people pull them apart. Pig Pickin's are comfortable in formal and informal crowds just as long as folks mind their BBQs. If you're in Down East, NC, with one, DO NOT mention ketchup. Pig Pickin's are most compatible with Sweet Teas and Mint Juleps.

PEACH COBBLER

(SEPTEMBER 23–OCTOBER 22)
What would a party be without a Peach Cobbler? Always filled with a choice bit of juicy morsels, gossips can't get enough of them. Males born under this sign can seem a little crusty, but don't be fooled by the tough exterior—they're sweet as pie on the inside!

COVERED DISH

(OCTOBER 23–NOVEMBER 22)
Covered Dishes spend a lot of their free time at Sunday service, so they tend to be more spiritual. Not only do they pray hard, they play hard. Unfortunately, they don't always love the one they're with. They often wake up at someone else's house, and some take their good ole time returning home. Still, no matter what the occasion—funeral, birth, wedding, new neighbors—you're comforted having Covered Dishes around.

LONGLEAF PINE

(NOVEMBER 23–DECEMBER 21)
Longleaf Pines make strong roots in the community, so everybody looks up to them. But, boy, do they know how to needle. Just ask their neighbors. They're not exactly strong in their convictions; they blow whichever way the wind does. Since they prefer to hang with their own, Longleaf Pines are best matched with other Longleaf Pines.

REBEL

(DECEMBER 22–JANUARY 20)
Rebels have a great sense of humor, but you don't want to cross them. Southerners born under this sign have a deep commitment to the past and don't like ch-ch-changes. Yankees born under this sign are rebels without a cause, but rebels just the same.

BUTTERMILK BISCUIT

(JANUARY 21–FEBRUARY 19)
Buttermilk Biscuits crave attention; they love when you butter 'em up. A little flaky, yes, but always crowd pleasers. There's something just a little bit old-fashioned about Buttermilk Biscuits. In fact, they often remind people of their grandmothers. Problem with partnering with a Buttermilk Biscuit is that it's hard to have just one.

MINT JULEP

(FEBRUARY 20–MARCH 20)
Mint Juleps, while a little prissy, really know how to liven up a party. From the Kentucky Derby to a debutante ball, Mint Juleps have a way of making everything (and everyone) look better. They're best with Covered Dishes and Pig Pickin's, but if you really want to make it interesting, pair a Mint Julep and a Rebel. Too many Mint Juleps in one night, though, and you can count on a headache.

Chapter 3

# Easy for You to Say

***You know that feeling you get*** when you first step on the tarmac in a foreign country? Part awe, part "What did I get myself into?" You get the same feeling when you move from north to south. You should have to clear customs. And in a manner of speaking, you do just that. At least there's no foreign language to master. But it helps to speak Southern to get along in the South. And all it takes is practice. Start by familiarizing yourself with the greetings.

## Snappy Southern Greetings

Yankees don't take it personally when someone on the bus doesn't say hello to them. In fact, we prefer your silence. Southerners, on the other hand, make a living of being friendly and would never pass someone on the street without engaging him in conversation. These snappy Southern greetings may take a little getting used to:

- **"Ya'll ain't from around here, are ya?"** (Like "Aloha," this is used interchangeably to say hello and good-bye.)

"Y'all ain't from around here, are ya?" is basically a rhetorical question. They know you ain't. Sometimes Southerners just want to have some fun with you. Pay attention to tone. This greeting can be hearty and playful or about as friendly as a doberman pinscher greeting you at the gate. You'll know it when you hear it.

- **"You sound like the Nanny!"**

Brooklyn, Chicago, Philadelphia: These accents all sounds the same to Southerners. Before you go home and wash your mouth out with soap, remind yourself that *The Nanny* made millions on her bad accent. What's stopping you?

- **"You're from New York, aren't ya?"**

This greeting is not about your accent; it's about your attitude. If you tend to speak without being spoken to or—gasp—skip the pleasantries and get right down to business, you're considered pushy, so probably a New Yorker. And your fifteen minutes of fame are up.

Southerners do have some greetings that don't nail down your place of birth.

- **"Hi, y'all."** (pronounced with three syllables)

Politically correct, proper, and friendly, "hi, y'all" has it all. It's equally at home at a governor's ball and a pig pickin'.

- **"Hey."** (pronounced with two syllables)

Even some Southerners find "hi y'all" a little too, well, Southern.

☆ ☆ ☆ ☆ ☆ ☆ ☆ ☆ ☆

## *Greetings You Will Never Hear from a Southerner*

"Wassup?"
"Hey, you guys!"
"Homey!"
"Yo, bro'!"

## *Ten Polite Ways to Put a Yankee in His Place*

1. "Here to stay or just visitin'?"
2. "I don't reckon I know your daddy."
3. "So you're one of those big-city girls."
4. "How do *you* like _____ (name of Southern city)?"
5. "Where are you from?"
6. "What brings you here?"
7. "Where were you born?"
8. "Do you work for IBM?" (I've Been Moved)
9. "Bet you miss the cold."
10. "Well, *our* ___ (library, grocery store, florist, fireworks display, art museum, etc.) isn't on the scale of what you might be accustomed to, but *we* love it."

Yankees find it much easier to understand Southerners when they learn to listen to what is not being said. For Southerners, minding your manners trumps telling the truth. "Tell it like it is" is not a badge of honor down here. Since Southerners don't always mean what they say, and don't always say what they mean, beginning listeners tend to lose some things in the translation.

## *The Berlitz Translation Guide to Communicating with Southerners*

| *What Southerners Say* | *What Southerners Mean* |
|---|---|
| Y'all come back and see us real soon now. | This conversation is over. |
| My mama taught me to never... | My manners are better than your manners. |
| Why, your potato salad is so original looking! | Your potato salad looks as if you digested it first. |
| I don't care for ________. | I &*$#'n hate ________. |
| Amber Leigh, bless her heart, made the casserole. | The casserole sucks! |
| We do things a little differently down here. | We don't give a rat's ass how you did it back home. |

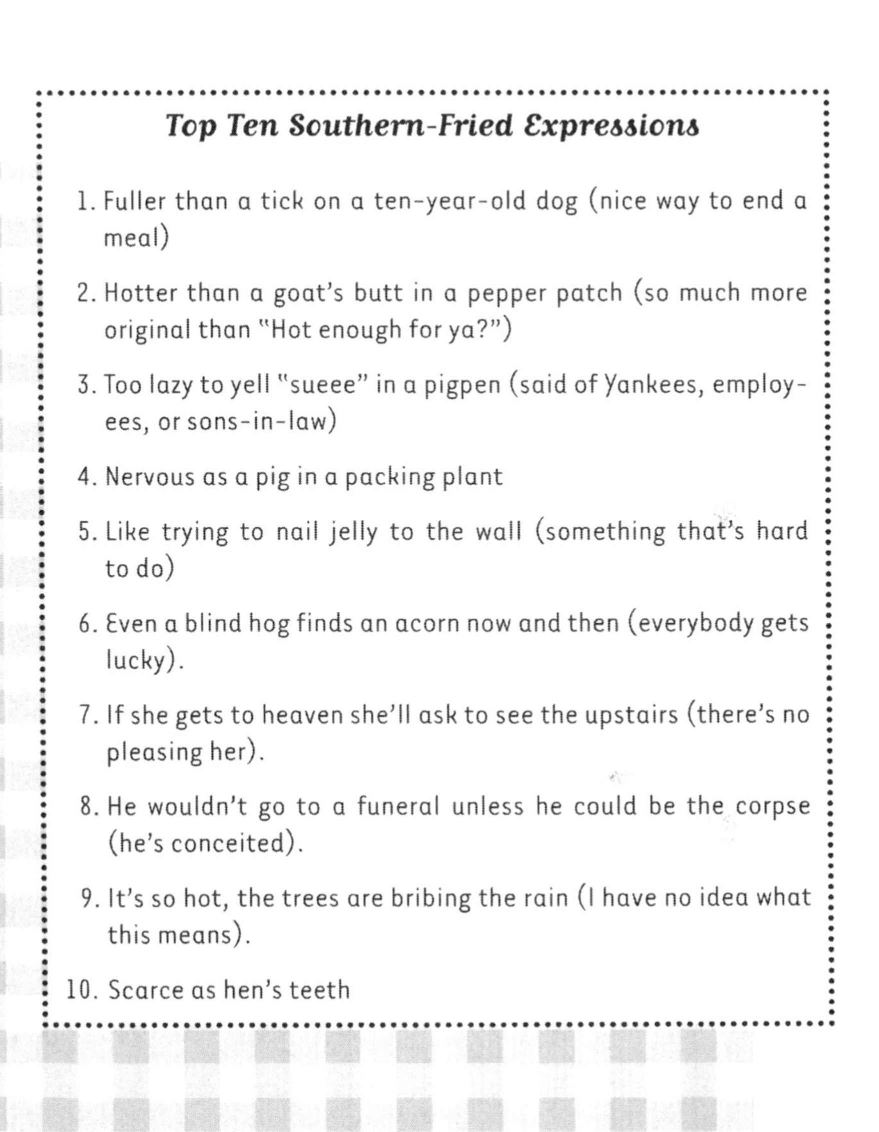

### *Top Ten Southern-Fried Expressions*

1. Fuller than a tick on a ten-year-old dog (nice way to end a meal)
2. Hotter than a goat's butt in a pepper patch (so much more original than "Hot enough for ya?")
3. Too lazy to yell "sueee" in a pigpen (said of Yankees, employees, or sons-in-law)
4. Nervous as a pig in a packing plant
5. Like trying to nail jelly to the wall (something that's hard to do)
6. Even a blind hog finds an acorn now and then (everybody gets lucky).
7. If she gets to heaven she'll ask to see the upstairs (there's no pleasing her).
8. He wouldn't go to a funeral unless he could be the corpse (he's conceited).
9. It's so hot, the trees are bribing the rain (I have no idea what this means).
10. Scarce as hen's teeth

### *Ten Ways to Say "Now That's Ugly" in Dixie*

1. Uglier than homemade soup (alternate: uglier than homemade soap).
2. He's so ugly his mother had to borrow a baby to take to church.
3. Ugly as a mud fence in a rainstorm.
4. So ugly she'd run a dog off a meat wagon.
5. Give me a fly flapper, and I'll help you kill it.
6. Looks like she's been hit in the face with a bag full of nickels.
7. He's so ugly he has to slap himself to sleep.
8. She's so ugly she has to sneak up on a glass of water to get a drink.
9. He's so ugly they had to tie a pork chop around his neck so the dog would play with him.
10. He looks like something the cat drug in and the dog wouldn't eat.

★ ★ ★ ★ ★ ★ ★ ★ ★

## *Southern Parts of Speech*

Traditional grammar teaches us eight parts of speech: nouns, verbs, pronouns, adjectives, adverbs, interjections, conjunctions, and prepositions. But Southerners would be lost without one more: palliatives. When Southerners want to contradict, take a shot at someone, or strongly disagree, they always open with a palliative or a piece of humble pie. Of course, their manner will stay soft and gentle, but when clause 1 starts with a maybe, clause 2 will always pack a punch.

- Am I wrong in thinking . . . (we should fire the whole staff)?
- I may be mistaken, but . . . (I think that's the worst hairdo I've ever seen).
- I'm not sure, but I believe . . . (these people against the president are uncivilized and anti-America).
- I should think . . . (anyone with even a basic understanding of history would know we actually won the war).

### *Yankee Don't Say!*

And I thought Philly was humid.
Are they kidding flying that Confederate flag in the town square?
I'm a yellow dog Democrat.
*Rawley* . . .
Don't any black people belong to this club?
I don't care for Southern cooking.
I'm here to stay.

### May I Help You?

Whether you're at the makeup counter or the home improvement store, you can expect service with a smile. No matter how bad the news. Southerners tend to smile broadest when they *can't* help you. When they don't have what you're looking for, the answer is "We surely don't," followed by a big smile. When you ask, "Do you know where I can get . . ." the answer more often than not is "I surely don't" followed by another giant grin.

## The A to Z Guide for Building Your Vocabulary or, The Dixie Dictionary (Abridged)

**All y'all** Plural for *you;* All y'alls—plural possessive
*Usage* We're awful sorry that *all y'all* are without power six days after the ice storm.
We're awful sorry that *all y'alls* electricity has been out for six weeks now.
(Approved by 90 percent of the Usage Panel; approved by only 3 percent of the people stuck without power)

**Butterbeans, boiled peanuts, or buttermilk biscuits** Don't ask a Southerner to choose a favorite food that begins with b.
*Usage* Pass the b ___s, please.

**Christian** In addition to God-fearing, "Christian" is used to describe a person who abstains from alcohol.
*Usage* "Open bar? Why, no, dear. We're *Christian.*" Also used in marketing to sell products. See the Yellow Pages for the Christian nearest you.

**Dadgumit** Socially acceptable expletive; "damn" in other languages.
*Usage* (Note: No need to watch your grammar when you're all fired up):
"Them Yankees is moving down here in droves, *dadgumit.*"
Or if you're really steamed:
"*Dadgum!* Mama done ate the last *dadgum* jar of *dadgum* pear preserves, *dadgumit.*"

**Everwhichaway** Hard to pinpoint location, may explain poor planning of the roads.
*Usage* "Oh, the Inner/Outer Beltline isn't north, south, east, or west, it goes *everwhichaway.*" Or "I dropped a bag o' boiled peanuts, and they went *everwhichaway.*"

**Fixin'** What you're going to do: derivative of *fix*—what you're doing.
*Usage* "We're *fixin'* to come over in about twenty minutes." (If this is your builder speaking, he's lying. He's *fixin'* to leave town.) Compare to fix:
"I'll *fix* dinner directly" (directly is a unit of time).
*Combined Usage:* "I'm *fixin'* to *fix* this here roof by tomorrow."

**Grits** World's eighth wonder. Ground corn meets religion when you see how much Southerners worship this mushy delicacy served 24/7. (Think Quaker Oatmeal on corn.)
*Usage* With butter at breakfast, with cheese at dinner, sliced and fried for leftovers

**Hadn't ought** Should not. Not to be confused with the multiple modal "might ought."
*Usage* "You *hadn't ought* to bother your sister like that." "You might ought give me a rest, dadgumit."

**Ill** A state of mild irritation for Southerners.
*Usage* "That *Beverly Hillbillies* reality show, it makes me right *ill.*"

**June bugs** Giant, gross-looking beetles that bang against the screen door in the spring looking to come in.
*Usage* Damaging lawns and scaring adults. Getting one tangled in your hair is reason to "go to pieces."

**Kudzu** A.k.a. "the vine that ate the South," "mile-a-minute vine," "foot-a-night vine"—you get the idea: It's green and it's out of control.
*Usage* Fry and eat (make a quiche), arts and crafts (make a basket), homeopathic meds (make a cure).

**Laying up** Loafing, doing nothing.
*Usage* "He's *laying up* till the big game on Saturday" (big game = college football).

**Marshal** Escort for the debutante at her ball.
*Usage* Two marshals per deb; marshal #1 gives his left arm, marshal #2 supports her left elbow for an easy glide into society.

**Nabs** Peanut butter crackers. The real Nabs (Nabisco's 1928 peanut sandwich packet) have been long gone, but don't tell that to the current generation of Southerners who insist they grew up on them. Southerners never forget their first Nab.
*Usage* Nabs and a Co'Cola (the small bottle, of course) perfect for a trip down memory lane: the snack reward at the end of tobacco row; in the brown-bag lunch Mama packed; while operating heavy machinery.

**Ought** Used instead of *should,* in combination with *should,* or paired with just about anything for emphasis, for example: *shouldn't ought, might ought, ought to could.* See "*hadn't ought.*"
*Usage* "I *ought* to go now. I *shouldn't ought* to stay this late on a school night."

**Pig Pickin'** A whole pig is slow-roasted over an open pit, and guests gather round and serve themselves, that is, pick the pig. Now, there's a party! Add some sides—coleslaw, hush puppies, baked beans, sweet tea, and banana pudding—and Southerners are happy as a pig in, uh, pick.
*Usage* "The senator will be at Saturday's *pig pickin'* if he knows what's good for him."

**Quilt** As with all things quaint, Southerners think they invented quilts. And Grandmaw's patchwork would make a believer out of anyone.

**RC Cola** The cola of choice for Southerners. Launched in the 1930s as Royal Crown Cola, Southerners affectionately called it RC, a nickname that stands today.
*Usage* Best served with a MoonPie (chocolate marshmallow snack).

**Slack-twisted** Lacking courage or shirking responsibility.
*Usage* "I wouldn't vote for him no way, no how; that *slack-twisted,* sorry fellow would steal a chaw of tobacco out of your mouth if you yawned."

**Texas T-shirts** The disposable toilet seat covers found in roadside bathrooms.
*Usage* With khakis or cutoffs; do not launder.

**Uppity** Stuck up.
*Usage* "I'm right tired of these *uppity* Yankees treating us like we're from the backwoods."

**Verandah, Veranda** Large Southern porch, usually roofed and sometimes enclosed, always tastefully furnished.
*Usage* Refined way of receiving guests without having to clean the house.

**Whopper-jawed** Crooked, askew; a.k.a. whomper-jawed, wappajawed, whoppy-jawed, whompey-jawed, whompsey-jawed, whata? jawed and even lopper-jawed.
*Usage* "And then I tell this dadgum computer to go ahead and print, and it's whopper-jawed."

**eXcusing** Except.
*Usage* "Your new house is finished, ma'am, *excusing* a few incidentals" ("incidentals" include the screens, doors that close, and holes in the wall).

**Y'all** Singular for "you" (Southerners will beg to differ here. They insist that even though they use it to address one person, it *implies* plurality.)

**"In their own words":** "Y'all is about five; all y'all's a bigger crowd; all y'all is for questions, not for statements."
*Usage* "Y'all ain't from around here, are ya?" (read: not just you but all you Yankees)

**Zoysia** A perennial Southern grass that loves the heat and humidity.
*Usage* Enjoy your grass all year-round (just like college!).

★ ★ ★ ★ ★ ★ ★ ★ ★

## A Yankee Defined

During the Civil War, Southerners referred contemptuously to all Northerners as Yankees. But in today's South, a Yankee is anyone who "ain't from around here." One can come from Chicago, Utah, Arizona, and California, too.

The origin of the term "Yankee" is still disputed. It's been said that the original Yankees were actually Dutch, and the term was first applied to the Dutch pirates in the Caribbean in the 1680s. When the Dutch settled in New England, the name started to be used for all New Englanders. During the American Revolution, the British jeeringly called American colonists Yankees and sang "Yankee Doodle Dandy" just to razz them. But after the Minutemen beat the pulp out of King George and his men at Lexington and Concord, the colonists started singing "Yankee Doodle" themselves, and it became the swan song for the British.

### Southern Terms of Endearment

Yankee dime: a kiss

Yankee shot: belly button (where the Yankee shot at ya and missed)

Yankeeland: the North

Yankee vegetables: undercooked greens (Southerners simmer theirs all day)

Yankee tea: urine

## *Mind Games*

**Anagram Directions: Can you find 20 words in**

# SOUTHERN HOSPITALITY?

(Today's contestants: The Damn Yankee vs. the Native Son or Daughter)

| *Damn Yankee* | *Native Son* |
|---|---|
| South | Royal |
| Phonies | South |
| Hostile | Posh |
| Trap | Party |
| No shops | Host |
| Help! | His 'N' Hers |
| Pity | Hi-Tea |
| Poseur | Stars |
| Sushi | Haute |
| No Hope | Spirit |
| Hot | The pool |
| Tar | Palatial |
| Hoity-toity | Photo op |
| Hail | Spatial |
| Typhoons | Plays |
| Loopy | Super |
| Pits | Tops |
| Split | Operas |
| Tailspin | Style |
| Stop | Southern Lit |
| These nuts | It rules! |

Chapter 4

☆ ☆ ☆ ☆ ☆ ☆ ☆ ☆ ☆

# Dressed to Kill

**Southerners dress to** *fit in,* not to *stand out.* So "reformed Yankees," you may have some changing to do as far as dressing for the role. Color-coordinated sweat suits aren't worn in public down here like they are up north. Southerners tend to kick it up a notch or two when they go out. And remember, we dress by the thermometer down here, not the calendar. So if it's a warm day in January, we're talking sundress and sandals, even if it was 40 degrees yesterday and an ice storm is predicted for tomorrow. (The Debs are the exception, of course. No white shoes after Labor Day and no velvet during the day. They don't care what the Weather Channel says.) Still want to dress the part? Let's take a stroll down the Southern catwalk to see what the Joneses are wearing.

## Daddy

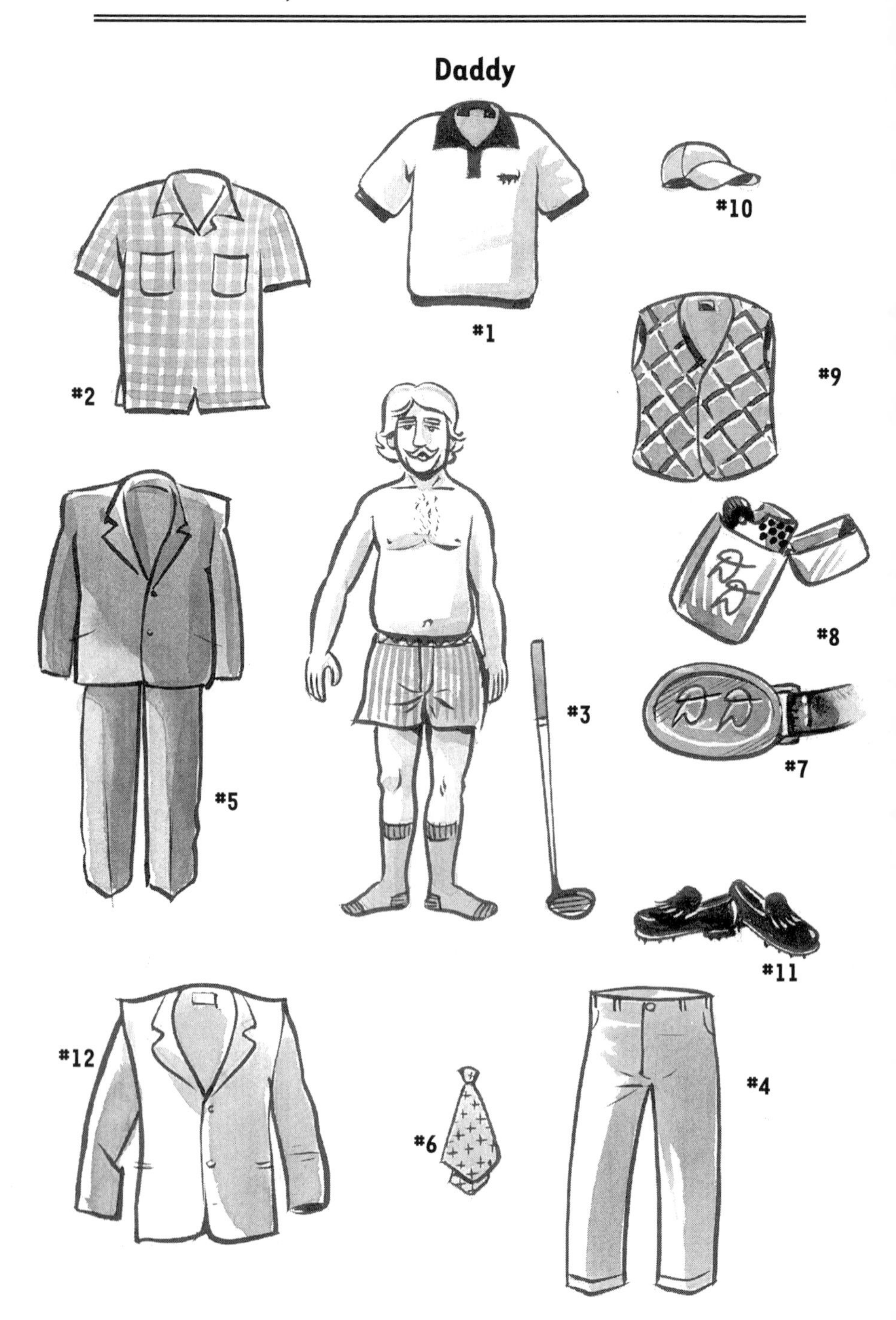

## *Daddy*

1. Pink golf shirt: Like their leading ladies, Southern gents love pastels.
2. Plaid or madras cotton short-sleeved shirt: You can never be too "cool" in the heat.
3. Golf club: Always "on call" for the links.
4. Khakis: Twelve months a year—and allegedly "wrinkle free."
5. Khaki or beige linen suit: This is the basic black of the South.
6. Wide tie: Never went out of style down here.
7. Sterling silver belt buckle with monogram: You *can* judge a man by his belt buckle.
8. Monogrammed lighter: Support our tobacco farmers, and do it with class.
9. Hunter orange vest: The buck stops here.
10. Pinehurst No. 2 golf cap: Even if you've never golfed it, you must pretend you did.
11. Golf shoes: If you only have one pair of shoes, it's got to be regulation.
12. White dinner jacket: Summer weddings for debs and friends of debs.

## Politico

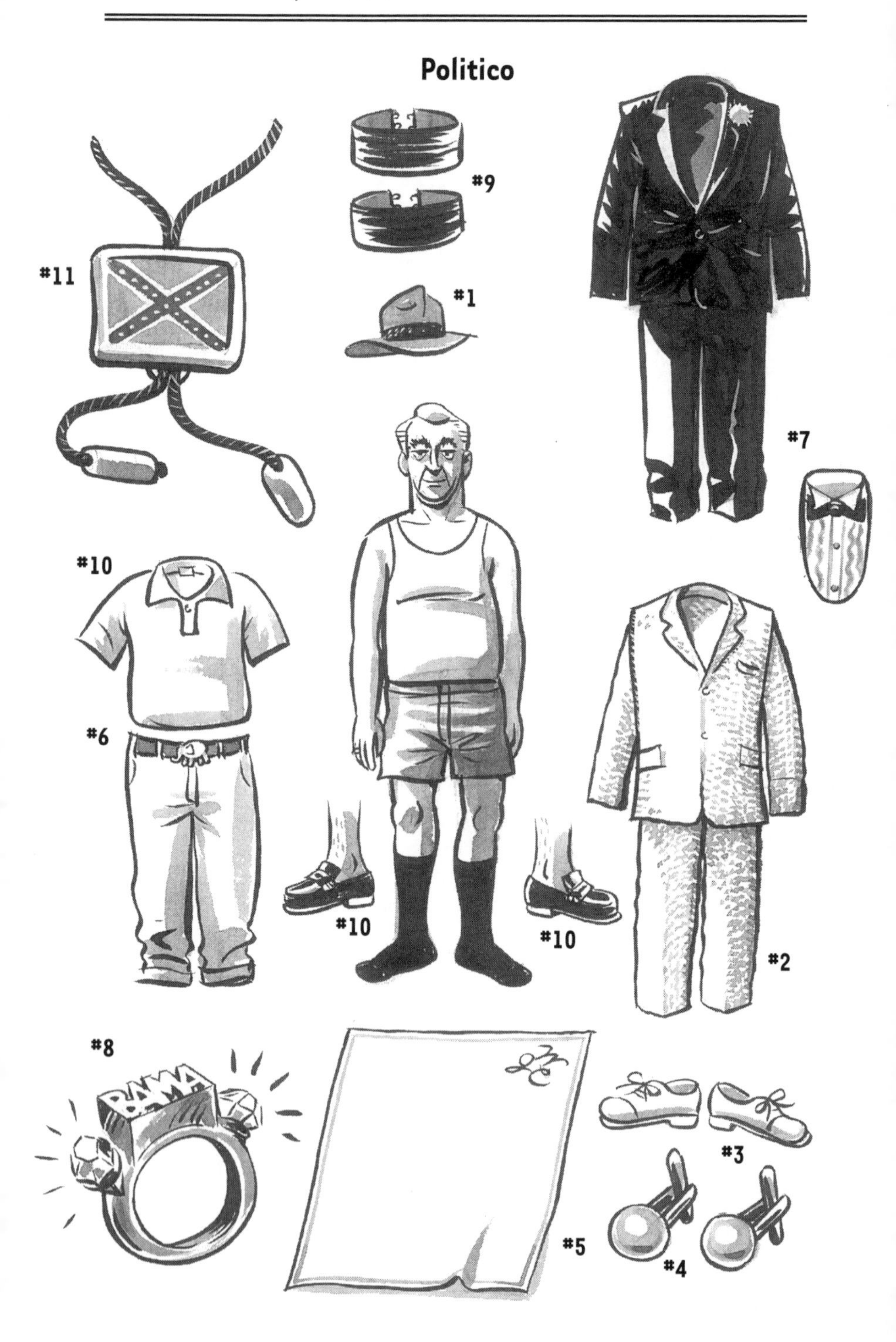

## Politico

1. Panama fedora: Derby Day, Mother's Day, Father's Day, can you say every day? This happening hat is worn with shorts, suits, and slacks—sport this bad boy with everything!
2. Seersucker suit: Blue, yellow, beige—you can't have just one. There's a seersucker born every minute.
3. White shoes: Gotta have them with a seersucker suit. Labor Day rules need not apply.
4. Black or white pearl cuff links: The free cloth cuff links that came with the shirt are too Democratic.
5. Monogrammed handkerchief: These come in handy for moving speeches (scandal apologies, etc.).
6. Republican elephant-shaped sterling silver belt buckle: This is the ultimate patriotic fashion statement.
7. Black tuxedo and white piqué wing-collar shirt: Rubber chicken never looked so good.
8. Class ring from any Southern school: If he didn't graduate, there's always the Robert E. Lee Confederate ring from the Franklin Mint.
9. Two satin cummerbunds: Hot pink and kelly green—real men wear brights.
10. Get-the-vote uniform: "Glad handing" outfit worn to meet and greet constituents—khakis, pastel golf shirt (unless PR gal mutes him), penny loafers, no socks, no undershirt (show the folks you're sweating for them).
11. Pewter bolo tie with Confederate battle flag: Worn with discretion—not to DC!

## Redneck

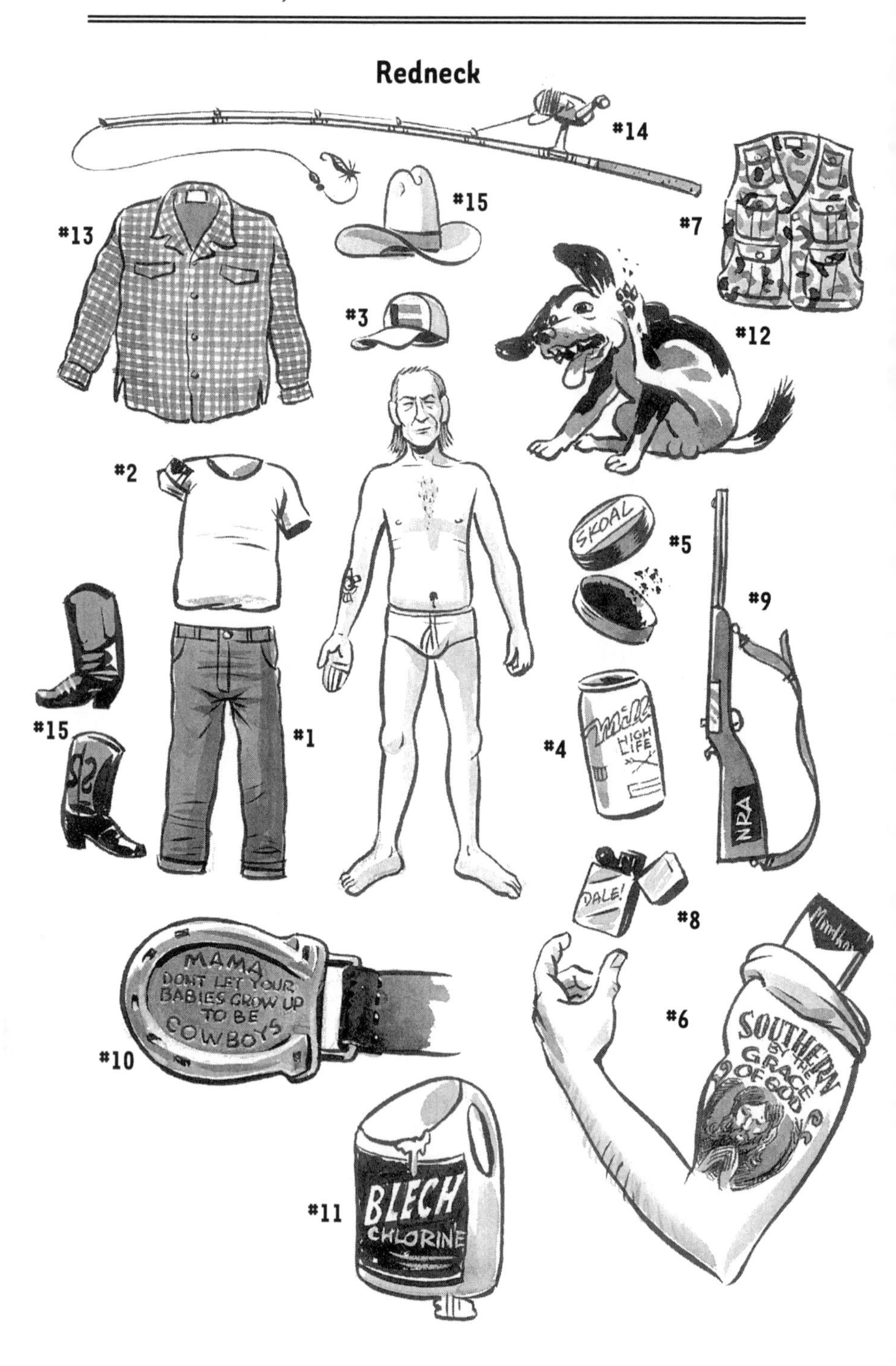
#14
#15
#7
#13
#3
#12
#2
SKOAL
#5
#9
#15
#1
Miller
HIGH
LIFE
#4
NRA
DALE!
#8
MAMA
DONT LET YOUR
BABIES GROW UP
TO BE
COWBOYS
#10
#6
SOUTHERN
BY THE
GRACE
OF GOD
#11
BLECH
CHLORINE

## Redneck

1. Jeans: Wash and wear, or don't wash and still wear.
2. T-shirt: Sleeve rolled up to hold pack of cigarettes—Marlboro or Camel.
3. Stars & Bars trucker hat: This emblem not to be confused with the battle flag emblem. He'll wear that tomorrow.
4. Can of Miller High Life: Empties are used for pee cans.
5. Skoal's wintergreen chewing tobacco: Nothing better than a chew in his cheek.
6. Monogrammed muscles
7. Camouflage hunting vest, 22 pockets: Dressed to kill.
8. Dale Earnhardt Black Ice Zippo Lighter: Father's Day present from his old girlfriend.
9. Hunting rifle, 44.40 caliber: God love the NRA.
10. Black leather belt with silver-plated belt buckle: Holds up his jeans.
11. Spit cup: Cutting off the top of a chlorine bleach jug and filling it with sawdust works in a pinch.
12. Hunting dog: "Bear," named after Bear Bryant.
13. Red plaid flannel shirt: A.k.a. the winter coat.
14. Rod & reel: A bad day fishin' is better than a good day working.
15. Cowboy gear: Big hat and big boots.

## Southern Belle

## *Color Me Beautiful (and Southern)*

Think pretty in pink, perfect in peach, and lovely in lilac. Not to mention flower power! Southern women just say no to blacks, browns, grays, and taupes.

## *Southern Belle (a.k.a. Daddy's Little Girl or The Deb)*

1. Wide-brimmed straw hat with chiffon-scarf tie: The look wouldn't be complete without the right hat at the right time.
2. Strapless sundress: Think poplin, think flowers, think feminine.
3. Peach blouse: Sweet as a Georgia peach—or is she?
4. Long silk skirt: Pastel or floral, loose fitting, not body hugging.
5. Modest, tasteful bathing suit, sophisticated beach cover-up, and trashy beach novel.
6. Straw bag with embroidery and pink lining: See contents at the end of this chapter.
7. Charm bracelet: Charm from ballet, debutante ball, finishing school, graduation, a little piggy from the annual pig pickin', a horse for riding lessons, a hair dryer, etc.
8. Hair bow: No ponytail should be without.
9. Sandals, the shoe of choice: Heels are great, but they tend to sink in the mud.
10. Flip-flops with flowers and/or beads: Not your mother's flip-flops—or are they?
11. Ladies' twill golf visor: Golfing with daddy is her favorite sport.
12. Debutante gown: Keepsake from the big night.
13. Sorority key: Opens so many doors for her.

## Daughter of the Confederacy

#6

#8

#4

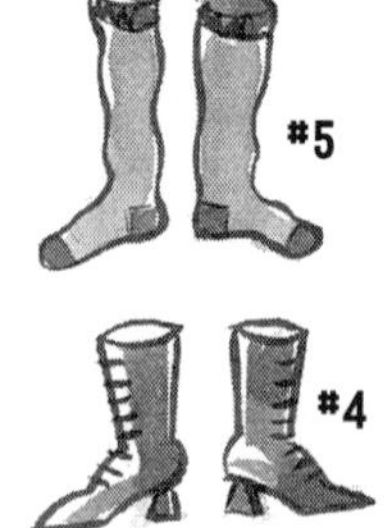

#11

## *Daughter of the Confederacy*

1. Khakis: The black slacks of the South.
2. Khaki skirt: Sensible in the heat, below the knee, of course.
3. Clutch purse: Girls will be girls—it must match the shoes.
4. Civil War reenactor uniform (simple dress, detachable white collar and cuffs, petticoat, corset, granny boots).
5. Knee-hi pantyhose: Lose the garter of yesteryear.
6. Rain bonnet: It will keep the weekly 'do in shape in case of downpour.
7. Denim sundress with embroidered flowers on collar.
8. Umbrella for rain—and shine (to keep the sun out of her eyes).
9. Tennis shoes—not sneakers, mind you.
10. Cotton floral-print cap sleeve tee with kick pleat chino skirt: For special occasions.
11. Red, white, and blue carnation corsage for special occasions.

★ ★ ★ ★ ★ ★ ★ ★ ★

## Mrs. Redneck

## Mrs. Redneck

1. Jeans, tight fitting; overalls are so last year.
2. Jeans miniskirt: Show some leg.
3. Camouflage blouse: You never know when you'll want to sneak up on your old man.
4. Halter top: For fun in the sun or a lark in the dark.
5. Camo shorts and/or camo cargo pants: Wear your honey's or buy your own.
6. Cutoff jeans: No such thing as too short.
7. White top with glitter graphics: Stars & Bars are always nice.
8. Hibiscus halter-top bikini top: Wear it with shorts.
9. Trucker hat for camouflage on bad-hair days.
10. Ankle-strap platforms with mud on the heels: Traveled a lot of miles of bad road.
11. Tennis-shoe slides—D.I.Y.: Cut off the back of a regular pair of tennis shoes.
12. Exchanged tattoos instead of "I do's."

★ ★ ★ ★ ★ ★ ★ ★ ★

## Southern Hair Dos

**His:** Mullet (blond, dirty blond, brown, or dirty brown); military buzz; bouffant (think televangelist); comb-over; puffy pompadour (premature gray or mature gray)

**Hers:** Ponytail with big bow; the frosted flirty flip (Southerners prefer blondes); vacuum-molded bouffant*; beehive (blue dye optional)

**Bouffant hairdos are also known as B-52's in the South (The rock group the B-52's took this hairdo in vain.)*

## *Hat Tips*

***To tip your hat or not to tip your hat . . . that is the question.***

1. Men are no longer required (but oh so welcome) to tip their hats to ladies.
2. Men *are* required to remove their hat during the National Anthem; women are not. (At first blush, this may seem unfair. But think about it. Men don't have to remove ribbons, flowers, bows, hairpins, oops, hair extensions, you get the idea.)
3. Some gents remove their hats in elevators. A plus, not a must.
4. Ladies keep their hats on indoors, especially ladies who lunch. (Men remove them.)
5. Ladies keep their hats on in church; men do not. Jewish men are the exception to the rule.
6. Men pin left; women pin right (when decorating the hatband).
7. Remove daytime hats at dusk.
8. Emily Post said to tip your hat to strangers, not friends, and to lift it for your wife.
9. If a man speaks to a woman on the street, he should remove his hat. (Once they start walking together, all hats are on.)
10. Cowboys say that to tip your hat to a man is to call him a woman. And that's a bad thing.

## *What's in a Yankee's Purse versus What's in a Southerner's Purse?*

| **Yankee** | **Southerner** |
| --- | --- |
| Subway card | Nabs |
| Sweet 'N Low | Smelling salts |
| Kleenex | Hand-embroidered handkerchief |
| Raving Red lipstick | Pretty in Peach lipstick |
| Birth control pills | Sterling silver monogrammed pillbox |
| Parking tickets | Grandma's coin purse |
| Checkbook | Dance card |
| Barneys charge card | Daddy's charge card |
| Cell phone | Black book |
| Mace (for unwanted thugs) | OFF! (for unwanted bugs) |
| Hair scrunchy | Heirloom hairpins |
| Broadway ticket stub | Peach cobbler recipe |

## *What's in a Yankee's Briefcase versus What's in a Southerner's Briefcase?*

| **Yankee** | **Southerner** |
|---|---|
| Laptop | Vienna sausage |
| 20 BICs (10 lighters, 10 pens) | Nabs |
| Legal pad | Wild Turkey, Jack Daniel's, or Jim Beam |
| Granola bar or sports bar | Holy Bible |
| Parking tickets | Waffle House VIP card (one more hole punch for a free waffle) |
| Alimony checks | Bait |
| Business cards | Hunting license |
| Tic Tacs | Smith & Wesson |
| Yesterday's sports page | NCAA pool |
| *Sports Illustrated* | *Field and Stream* |

One bright July morning, you'll drive to Wal-Mart, park your car, and enjoy shopping in air-conditioned comfort. But when it comes time to leave the store and cross the shimmering sea of cars baking in the noonday heat, you'll need your

### *How-to-Walk-from-the-Store-Back-to-the-Car without-Dying, Fun-in-the-Sun Survival Kit*

1. Bottled water
2. Fruit (shelf life: 20 minutes; goes from not ripe to ripe to overripe to bad before you get home from the grocery store)
3. Loose-fitting, light-colored clothes (You'll need a change of clothes after your "workout.")
4. Wide-brimmed straw hat (trucker hats for men) for shade
5. Cell phone so your fairy godmother can call 9-1-1 when you black out
6. Parasol or umbrella
7. Wet towel
8. Suntan lotion
9. Water spritzer
10. A watermelon—may be a little cumbersome, but you'll have something to share with fellow Yankees in distress

Chapter 5

# No Grits, No Glory

***If you're looking for comfort food,*** you've come to the right place. If you're all about healthy eating, you're going to have to lighten up. Make that fatten up. It's been said that the four basic food groups in the South are beans, bacon, whiskey, and lard. Yes, the salads are more grease than green (a side salad means potato salad or coleslaw), but come on; real Yankees don't have much room to talk.

## The Food Pyramid

### Fats, Oils, & Sweets (use sparingly)

| Yankee | Southerner |
| --- | --- |
| Sparingly means "Spare no expense; we'll pay anything for extra-virgin olive oil." | Sparingly means "Pass me the lard, and spare me the lecture." |

*(continued on next page)*

### *Milk, Yogurt, and Cheese (2–3 servings)*

| **Yankee** | **Southerner** |
|---|---|
| Skim latte | Buttermilk biscuits |
| Cheesesteak | Bacon and cheese grits |
| Goat cheese pizza | Boiled custard |

### *Vegetable Group (3–5 servings)*

| **Yankee** | **Southerner** |
|---|---|
| Bloody Mary (three) | Fried green tomatoes |
| Zucchini bread | Butterbean casserole |
| New Jersey tomatoes | Mint Julep (greens, right?) |
| | Corn pudding |
| | Sweet potato pie |

### *Meat, Poultry, Fish, Dry Beans, Eggs, and Nuts (2–3 servings)*

| **Yankee** | **Southerner** |
|---|---|
| Scrambled eggs and scrapple | Praline pecan pie |
| Sushi | Bucket of the Colonel's |
| TastyKake's Peanut Butter KandyKakes | Boiled peanuts |

## Fruit
## (2–4 servings)

| Yankee | Southerner |
|---|---|
| Banana split | Peach cobbler (2 slices) |
| Chocolate-covered cherries | Key lime pie |

## Bread, Cereal, Rice, and Pasta
## (6–11 servings)

| Yankee | Southerner |
|---|---|
| Bagel and cream cheese | Hush puppies |
| Chocolate granola bar | Bread pudding |
| Soft pretzel | Jambalaya |
| Baguette | Grits |
| Pound of penne | Grits |
| 12-foot Italian hoagie | Grits |

✯ ✯ ✯ ✯ ✯ ✯ ✯ ✯ ✯

### *Who's Nuts?*

**Pecan Pronunciation Guide**

*Pee-KAHN (very Southern)*
*PEE-can (very Yankee)*
*Pee con (nice compromise?)*

You know it's hard if they're studying it at Harvard. How do people around the country pronounce pecan? And the survey says . . .

a. [pi:kæn] with stress on the first syllable ("PEE-can") (17.03%)
b. [pi:kæn] with stress on the second syllable ("pee-CAN") (9.02%)
c. [pi:kan] with stress on the first syllable ("PEE-kahn") (13.19%)
d. [pi:kan] with stress on the second syllable ("pee-KAHN") (28.60%)
e. [pi:kæn] ("pick-Ann") (1.48%)
f. [pi:kan] ("pick-Ahn") (20.92%)

*Source: Harvard University Dialect Survey*

## *Let's Give It Up for Winn-Dixie and Piggly Wiggly*

Ready for your first trip to the supermarket? You won't recognize the names of the stores or the products on their shelves, but the grocery stores here sell wine and beer, and that's got to count for something. Yankees tend to need a drink after cruising down all the unfamiliar aisles and coming up with an empty cart at the finish line. We search in vain for brands we recognize and comfort foods from home. Cheesesteaks, corn relish, au jus, Italian hoagies, escarole, Tasty-Kakes, bialys, nam pla, arugula, Mexican salted beef, kosher-for-Passover matzo: We're all looking for something different. Yet our varied inquiries all elicit the same cheerful and prompt response from the store manager: "Y'all not from around here, are ya?" or "Sure don't!"

Spare yourself the heartache by taking along this clip-and-save list for stocking your pantry.

## *Clip-and-Save Grocery List*

Poke salet (the young leaves of the poke weed)
Canned creecy greens (dryland watercress)
Collards
Okra
Pickled peaches
Pickled ramps (wild onions)
Chowchow (spicy pickled relish for the serious Southern cook)
Jerusalem artichoke relish
Mt. Olive Bread & Butter Pickles
Old South Okra Pickles
14 cans of Cream of Mushroom soup—one week's supply for casseroles
Whole white hominy
White and yellow cornmeal (cornmeal for grits comes in white or yellow—same as the two hair colors here)
Stone-ground grits
Quick grits (quick is so taboo, but lying about it is fine)
Hush puppy mix
Wonder Bread
Texas Pete
Tony Chachere's (your new Old Bay)
Duke's Mayonnaise (pronounced man-aze)
Bone Suckin' Sauce
Fig preserves
Buttermilk
Pimiento cheese
Cheese straws
Boiled peanuts
MoonPies
Nabs
Pork rinds

**Unanswered Questions:** I haven't seen a green tomato since I moved here. So what are they frying?

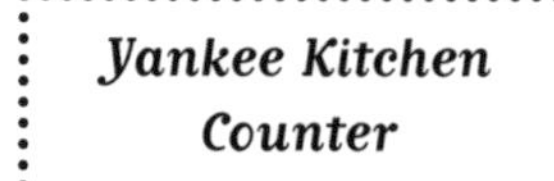

| *Yankee Kitchen Counter* | *Southern Kitchen Counter* |
| --- | --- |
| Coffee grinder | Cast-iron skillet |
| Martini shaker | Bacon drippings |
| Cascade | Raid |
| Pizza take-out menu | Deep-fat fryer |
| Power Bars | Mason jars |
| Spice rack | Gun rack |

## *Minding Your BBQs*

There are two religions down South: Baptist and Barbecue. And if you want to experience religious intolerance, try preaching the virtues of tangy spices and yellow mustard in a town that prides itself on its sweet tomato-ketchup-based barbecue. We can't help you avoid all the Yankee pit(s)falls, but we can help you avoid one. Here's what barbecue is not: something you do in the yard with hot dogs, chicken, and burgers. That's what we call a *cookout* down here. In the South, barbecue is meat soaked in sauce and slow cooked (slow like twenty-four hours) over the pit of a hardwood fire. With the notable exceptions of Texas and parts of Kentucky (states that aren't one bit sheepish about their mutton), the meat of choice is usually pork. It can be pulled, cut, shredded, chopped, sliced, or diced. But anyway you cut it, the meat is only part of the story. There's that controversial sauce that accompanies it. Your choice of sauce is the boldest decision you will make when you move south, and no Yankee author who wants to see tomorrow would point you in one direction and leave out another. You're on your own, partner.

**Using Barbecue in a Sentence**

**Yankee Don't! "*Jeet yet? Wanna barbecue some dogs?*"**

**Yankee Do! "*I love barbecue. I like ___ style best.*" (See town crier for the politically correct response.)**

## *Country Ham*

Southerners don't eat sissy, I mean city, hams; they eat country hams. Tennessee, Kentucky, and Virginia are country hams' "it" states, but don't say that in the Carolinas. The difference between a city and a country ham is in the curing, basically dry versus wet. (The moist slicing hams found in Yankee supermarkets are city hams.) Country hams are not fully cooked but dry cured to be safely stored at room temperature, and it's the particular method of curing and the length the ham is hung that give the country ham its distinctive taste. Umm. Salty. Ham connoisseurs in the South are like the coffee and wine snobs in the North. They insist it takes a sophisticated palate to prefer the more robust flavor—a skill that one masters over time. As with all of the finer things in life, it's important to have the right accouterment:

### Redeye Gravy Recipe

1 slice country ham
2 to 4 tablespoons strong brewed coffee
Optional: flour, water, sugar

Fry up one piece of country ham and remove from skillet. Add 2 to 4 tablespoons of brewed coffee to fat drippings. Pour gravy over ham, biscuits, and grits, and sop it up for a well-balanced Southern breakfast.

**Yield: 2 servings**

**Yankee Do! Soak a country ham in milk or water for several hours or overnight to reduce the saltiness. You're not being a wuss. Southerners do this, too.**

## *Happy New Year!*

Country ham is an absolute must for the traditional Southern New Year's Day meal. Southerners eat greens such as cabbage, collard greens, or kale to bring them money, and black-eyed peas with hog jowl to bring them luck. (The money-hungry add cornbread for extra wealth.)

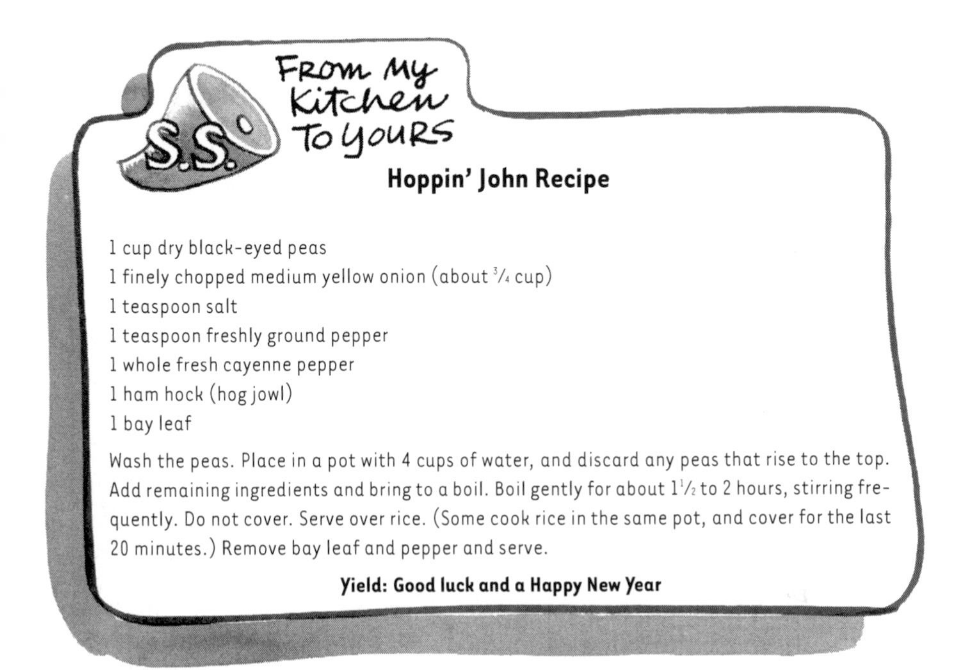


**Hoppin' John Recipe**

1 cup dry black-eyed peas
1 finely chopped medium yellow onion (about ¾ cup)
1 teaspoon salt
1 teaspoon freshly ground pepper
1 whole fresh cayenne pepper
1 ham hock (hog jowl)
1 bay leaf

Wash the peas. Place in a pot with 4 cups of water, and discard any peas that rise to the top. Add remaining ingredients and bring to a boil. Boil gently for about 1½ to 2 hours, stirring frequently. Do not cover. Serve over rice. (Some cook rice in the same pot, and cover for the last 20 minutes.) Remove bay leaf and pepper and serve.

**Yield: Good luck and a Happy New Year**

**Yankee Do! Buy your dry peas early, or your luck may run out! Fresh or frozen black-eyed peas will work in a pinch.**

## *Dining Out*

Southerners don't make a big thing out of their ethnicity: Italian, Irish, Polish, German, Scottish? Who cares? You're Southern, aren't you!?? So don't come looking for the old country in the form of quaint ethnic restaurants. If you see an ad for Mama Rose's, it's probably a coupon for a frozen dinner, not a trattoria. You'd be wise to forget "When in Rome." As far as location, location, location, can you see the beauty in strip malls instead of picturesque Roman piazzas? (Way less pigeons! Convenient shopping on the way back to the car!) Your anniversary dinner is likely to take place next door to a hardware store—you never know when you're going to need duct tape, now, do you? While décor in Southern restaurants tends toward shabby rather than chic, the good news is that big praying hands and checkered tablecloths never go out of style.

You'll never starve if you like meat and threes and fish camps. (Not to mention the hometown hero, Waffle House.) Jell-O, macaroni and cheese, and baked apples are just a few of the savory choices for your "threes." Seafood lover? You'll think something's a little fishy down here. Seafood restaurants are often called "fish camps." Camp, yes. Fish, maybe. In the South, you'll have no idea if you're eating shrimp, tuna, salmon, catfish, or crawfish. It's fried beyond recognition. And fresh means fresh frozen—just fried so you can't tell.

### *On the Menu*

**True Story!** My sister, visiting from the North, didn't know what to make of the Southern menu. A picky eater, bless her healthy heart, she was struggling with the unfamiliar choices (none of which sported the healthy heart insignia). Her only hope was the special.

"Are the crab cakes fried?" Denise asked, wincing.

The waitress beamed with Southern pride. "*Deep*-fat fried," she joyfully declared.

Denise stalled for time by taking a sip of her iced tea. I now know what a Yankee's face looks like when they first sample sweet tea. It's a cross between stifling a yawn with your mouth closed and receiving Botox injections around the lip. Where's a Long Island iced tea when you need one? Bon appetit, sis!

## *The Joy of Cooking (or Dining In)*

You might choose to take refuge in your own kitchen. But sooner or later, you're going to have to break bread (okay, biscuits) with the neighbors. Want to have the most popular dish at the potluck? No covered dish dinner in the South will turn you away carrying any of these:

- Buttermilk biscuits
- Sweet potato pie
- Red velvet cake
- Boiled custard

## *Deviled Eggs*

If you feel more comfortable making something you know, you can't go wrong with deviled eggs. Southerners seem to think they invented them, but the deviled eggs here are the same as the ones from home. There's just one Southern secret. It's not your mother's deviled egg plate. It's your *grand*mother's. Think heirloom. Deviled egg plates are so big in the South that they give them as wedding presents. If you hear someone talking excitedly about her designer, she's not talking about who created her purse; she's talking about her egg plate. *"It's a Gail Pittman!"*

### Deviled Eggs Recipe

6 large eggs
2 tablespoons mayonnaise
1 teaspoon prepared mustard (ballpark yellow for great color)
2½ tablespoons sweet pickle relish
⅛ teaspoon salt
dash of pepper
Garnish: paprika and/or parsley

Place eggs in a nonreactive saucepan and add enough cold water to cover by 3 inches. Bring to a boil. Reduce heat and simmer eggs for 15 minutes. Plunge eggs into cold water to prevent further cooking. To shell, tap each egg firmly on the counter until little cracks form, and then roll between your palms. Peel under cold running water.

Slice eggs lengthwise with a wet knife, and carefully remove yolks. Mash yolks with mayo. Add mustard, relish, salt, and pepper, and stir well. Spoon yolk mixture into egg whites, or go all out and use a pastry bag. Garnish if desired. Serve on designer egg plate or don't serve at all.

**Yield: 6 servings**

**Yankee Don't! Count calories down here.**

### *"Tomorrow Is Another Day" Calorie Counter*

| | Calories | Grams of Fat | % Calories from Fat |
|---|---|---|---|
| Pecan pie | 578 | 32 | 50 |
| Mac and cheese* (per serving, not per box!) | 1,230 | 60 | 49 |
| Southern fried chicken dinner (1 drumstick, 1 breast, coleslaw, fries, and a biscuit) | 1,000 | 56 | 50 |
| Krispy Kreme (1 chocolate iced, cream filled) | 350 | 21 | 54 |
| Mango key lime pie | 718 | 39 | 49 |

*Good grief: If your attendance is required or desired at a Southern funeral, it is customary to extend your condolences via a covered dish and dessert: mac and cheese or fried chicken and banana pudding.

**Yankee Do! Call them PRAH-leens or PRAW-leens, even PLA-reens, just don't call them PRAY-leens.**

## *Sweet Dreams*

Despite all your newfound guilty pleasures, if you're like most transplants, you'll be haunted in your sleep by the ones that got away. I dream of Philadelphia cheesesteaks, whitefish on a bagel from Hymie's, and Hope's chocolate milkshakes. My husband walks in his sleep looking for Carson's Ribs of Chicago. One Yankee friend experiences night shivers as she travels through time in search of her White Castle burger. Another yearns for his Skyline chili from Ohio. Someone else misses Jack In the Box. There's not a transplant in the world who never craves a taste from home.

So what keeps you up at night? Bet we can have it here by tomorrow. Here's a taste of takeout that should please any palate. But of course you'll want to see what your own city has to offer. Check the Web for the grocer nearest you!

Taste of Philadelphia: www.tasteofphiladelphia.com

Tastes of Chicago: www.tastesofchicago.com

Cincinnati To You: www.cincinnati-to-you.com

The New York First Company: www.newyorkfirst.com

Hometown Favorites: www.hometownfavorites.com

★ ★ ★ ★ ★ ★ ★ ★ ★

### *The Real Thing?*
### *or "Co-Cola"*

Coke was introduced in Atlanta the year it went dry (1866), and according to local lore (but still denied by the company), the real Classic Coke got a little help from its friends—cocaine was allegedly one of the original ingredients. One can just hear the clean-living Atlanta folks exulting, *"Hard liquor is so yesterday; I actually prefer these soft drinks!"* No wonder Southerners hold such a soft spot for Coke. Maybe that's why they call any carbonated beverage, regardless of flavor, a Coke. You rarely hear a Southerner use the terms "soda" or "pop." According to the Harvard University Dialect Study, Southerners are outnumbered on this one. Here's what people around the country call a carbonated beverage:

Soda: 54%
Pop: 24%
Coke: 12%

But who are we to say? Southerners lead the nation in the invention and consumption of carbonated beverages. They invented Pepsi, Dr Pepper, Mountain Dew, RC Cola, and Coca-Cola, and they consume about a jillion gallons a year.

## *Sweet Tea*

Southerners may love their "Cokes," but to them, Coke will never be the real thing. Their hearts belong to iced tea. Sweet tea for short. Emphasis on the sweet. It's never out of season here—Southerners down it by the bucket all year round. A note of caution to Yankees: If you go into any Southern restaurant and order iced tea, don't even think about adding your own packet of sugar. All iced tea is served pre-sweetened down here—at a ratio of about five pounds per glass. Yankees tend to go into sugar shock after one sip. If tea were sold like liquors—you know, 50 proof, etc.—sweet tea would be the grain alcohol of iced tea. Don't drink and drive.

### Sweet Tea Recipe

3 family-size tea bags or 8 regular tea bags (detach tags and string together for easy handling)
1⅓ to 1½ cups sugar
Optional: pinch of baking soda (add to hot brew to reduce bitterness and/or darken tea color)

Bring 4 cups of cold water to a rolling boil. Remove from heat and add tea bags. Steep in covered pot for six minutes. Use wooden spoon to squeeze excess liquid from tea bags before removing. Add sugar *while tea is hot,* stirring to dissolve. Pour into gallon pitcher, and add cold water (ice optional) to fill "tea jug" to capacity. Leave on counter for two reasons: 1. The fridge makes the tea cloudy. 2. Your kitchen will take on that *Southern Living* look. Serve tea by the glass over lots of ice. (The South is still divided on lemons, so serve them on the side.)

**Yield: One gallon (serves 2 Southerners or 16 Yankees)**

## *The Mint Julep*

Leaves in, leaves out, caster sugar, sugar syrup, straw or no straw, crush, layer, or muddle, the preparation of the mint julep is as personal to the Southern host as his or her barbecue sauce. Most can agree on shaved ice, bourbon, sugar, and mint. Silver cup or highball glass? Peppermint or spearmint? A dash of angostura bitters? Garnish with a mint leaf dipped in powdered sugar? A slice of lemon? Will the controversies never end? Just pour one!

From My Kitchen To Yours

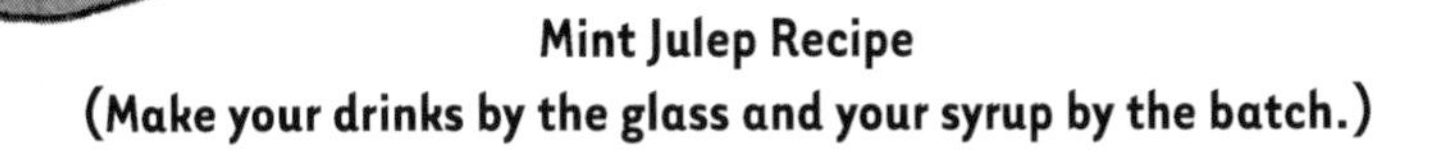

**Mint Julep Recipe**
**(Make your drinks by the glass and your syrup by the batch.)**

2 teaspoons sugar syrup
7 sprigs fresh mint (save one for garnish)
crushed ice
1 generous jigger Kentucky bourbon

Make a simple syrup by boiling equal parts water and sugar for five minutes. Fill a chilled silver julep cup (or highball glass if it's the best you can do) with syrup and mint. Crush the mint with the back of a spoon until the fragrance is released. Add bourbon and crushed ice, and stir rapidly to frost the outside of the cup. Garnish with mint sprig; add straw and serve.

**Yield: One serving**

**Yankee Do! If you want to be the mint julep queen, trim straws so they just peek out of the cup. The ultimate sip and sniff!**

# POSTCARDS FROM THE EDGE

### *Map of the South—Easy for You to Draw!*

*The South means different things* to different people. There's the South as defined by the Civil War—that includes any state that fought on the side of the Confederacy. There's the South that's bordered by the Mason-Dixon Line—the line designating the border between Pennsylvania, Maryland, and Delaware and dividing free states and slave states according to the Missouri Compromise of 1820. There's the South as shown on the presidential election maps—all the states in red—and, finally, there's the South as identified by the U.S. Census.

*Southern Living*, arguably a higher authority than the U.S. Census, defines the South as the seventeen states above, plus Missouri. We think Missouri tends to complicate things. We're still struggling to understand the Missouri Compromise. As far as our other options, well, the Mason-Dixon Line is *so two centuries ago*! And the Republican map is hard enough to look at during the elections.

In our humble opinion, the Census's definition of the South is the least divisive—even if it does divide the South into three regions. This list of the Southern states is the expressed view of the U.S. government and doesn't necessarily reflect that of the author. (But as you'll see, I couldn't resist a few unsolicited comments. Delaware? Maryland? DC? *Southern?* Oh, sweet mysteries of life.)

### *The South (as Defined by the U.S. Census)*

**(South Atlantic)**

Delaware (Be serious!)
Maryland (Talk about borderline.)
Washington, D.C. (Clearly a brand unto themselves.)
Virginia (I buy it.)
West Virginia (Even Southerners think these guys are hillbillies.)
North Carolina (I know this one from firsthand experience. Despite what the natives tell us, trust me, NC is Southern.)
South Carolina (Almost *too* Southern.)
Georgia (Southern as a Georgia peach.)
Florida (Get real, they really are all from New York.)

**(East-South Central)**

Kentucky (Southern all right.)
Tennessee (So, so Southern.)
Mississippi (Oh, yeah. Southern.)
Alabama (Southern to a fault.)

**(West-South Central)**

Oklahoma (No way. More like the mild, wild West.)
Arkansas (Unlike Missouri—that wishes it were Southern—Arkansas makes it by a hair [think pompadour].)
Louisiana (Cajun Southern.)
Texas (Like Gray Davis described California before they terminated him, Texas has people from every planet. It's the New York of the South.)

### *Ready for Their Close-up?*

### *Alabama (AL-uh-BAM-uh)*

**Nickname:** Yellowhammer State
**Capital City:** Montgomery
**State Motto:** *Audemus jura nostra defendere* (We dare defend our rights)
**State Flower:** Camelia
**State Bird:** Yellowhammer
**State Tree:** Longleaf pine
**State Song:** "Alabama"
**Famous Natives:** Courteney Cox Arquette, Nat "King" Cole, Zelda Fitzgerald, Harper Lee, Willie Mays, Rosa Parks
**What They Want You to Remember:** Bear Bryant
**What They Want You to Forget:** Every coach since

### *Arkansas (ARK-KIN-SAW)*

**Nickname:** The Natural State
**Capital City:** Little Rock
**State Motto:** *Regnant populus* (The people rule)
**State Flower:** Apple blossom
**State Bird:** Mockingbird
**State Tree:** Pine
**State Song:** "Arkansas"
**Famous Natives:** Maya Angelou, Bill Clinton, Glen Campbell, Johnny Cash, Douglas MacArthur
**What They Want You to Remember:** The Ozarks
**What They Want You to Forget:** Whitewater

## *Delaware (DEL-wore)*

**Nickname:** First State/Diamond State/Blue Hen State/Small Wonder *(Author's note to Delaware: Have you considered "Indecisive State"?)*
**Capital City:** Dover
**State Motto:** Liberty and Independence
**State Flower:** Peach blossom
**State Bird:** Blue hen chicken
**State Tree:** American holly
**State Song:** "Our Delaware"
**Famous Natives:** Valerie Bertinelli, E. I. du Pont, Henry Heimlich (voted most likely to maneuver), Caesar Rodney
**What They Want You to Remember:** Many people living there are descendants of the du Ponts.
**What They Want You to Forget:** They aren't one of them.

### *Florida (FLAR-dah)*

**Nickname:** Sunshine State
**Capital City:** Tallahassee
**State Motto:** In God We Trust
**State Flower:** Orange blossom
**State Bird:** Mockingbird
**State Tree:** Sabal palmetto
**State Song:** "Suwanee River"
**Famous Natives:** Pat Boone, Steve Carlton, Fay Dunaway, Jim Morrison, Sidney Poitier, Janet Reno
**What They Want You to Remember:** Di$ney World
**What They Want You to Forget:** Butterfly ballots and hanging chads

### *Georgia (JAW-ja)*

**Nickname:** Peach State
**Capital City:** Atlanta
**State Motto:** Wisdom, Justice, and Moderation
**State Flower:** Cherokee rose
**State Bird:** Brown thrasher
**State Tree:** Live oak
**State Song:** "Georgia on My Mind"
**Famous Natives:** Jimmy Carter, Ray Charles, Ty Cobb, Hulk Hogan, Martin Luther King, Jr., Margaret Mitchell, Burt Reynolds, Little Richard
**What They Want You to Remember:** The Confederate flag in the town hall
**What They Want You to Forget:** The Confederate flag in the town hall

## *Kentucky (CAIN-TUC-KEY)*

**Nickname:** Bluegrass State
**Capital City:** Frankfort
**State Motto:** United We Stand, Divided We Fall
**State Flower:** Goldenrod
**State Bird:** Kentucky cardinal
**State Tree:** Tulip poplar
**State Song:** "My Old Kentucky Home"
**Famous Natives:** Muhammad Ali, Abraham Lincoln, Loretta Lynn, Bill Monroe, Diane Sawyer
**What They Want You to Remember:** The Kentucky Derby
**What They Want You to Forget:** Kentucky Fried Chicken

### *Louisiana (LUZY-ANNA)*

**Nickname:** Pelican State
**Capital City:** Baton Rouge
**State Motto:** "Union, Justice, and Confidence"
**State Flower:** Magnolia
**State Bird:** Eastern brown pelican
**State Tree:** Bald cypress
**State Song:** "Give Me Louisiana," "You Are My Sunshine"
**Famous Natives:** Louis Armstrong, Geoffrey Beene, Truman Capote, Fats Domino, Bryant Gumbel, Lillian Hellman, Cokie Roberts
**What They Want You to Remember:** Mardi Gras
**What They Want You to Forget:** Getting robbed at Mardi Gras

### *Maryland (MER-lin, as in BALL-more, MER-lin)*

**Nickname:** Old Line State, Free State
**Capital City:** Annapolis
**State Motto:** *Fatti maschii, parole femine* (Strong Deeds, Gentle Words)
**State Flower:** Black-eyed Susan
**State Bird:** Baltimore oriole
**State Tree:** White oak
**State Song:** "Maryland! My Maryland"
**Famous Natives:** Spiro Agnew, John Wilkes Booth, Frederick Douglass, Billie Holiday, Francis Scott Key, Thurgood Marshall, Babe Ruth, Harriet Tubman, Frank Zappa
**What They Want You to Remember:** The Inner Harbor
**What They Want You to Forget:** The inner city

### *Mississippi (MIS-SIPPE)*

**Nickname:** Magnolia State
**Capital City:** Jackson
**State Motto:** *Virtute et armis* (By valor and arms)
**State Flower:** Magnolia
**State Bird:** Mockingbird
**State Tree:** Magnolia
**State Song:** "Go, Mississippi"
**Famous Natives:** Jimmy Buffett, Jim Henson, James Earle Jones, Elvis Presley, Tennessee Williams, Oprah Winfrey, Tammy Wynette
**What They Want You to Remember:** The King was born there.
**What They Want You to Forget:** The average Mississippian chews 112 pounds of tobacco per year.

### *North Carolina (NAWTH CA-LIN-AH)*

**Nickname:** Tar Heel State
**Capital City:** Raleigh
**State Motto:** *Esse quam videri* (To be rather than to seem)
**State Flower:** Dogwood
**State Bird:** Cardinal
**State Tree:** Pine
**State Song:** "The Old North State"
**Famous Natives:** Clay Aiken, David Brinkley, Howard Cosell, Roberta Flack, Ava Gardner, Andy Griffith, Andrew Johnson, Charles Kuralt, Soupy Sales
**What They Want You to Remember:** Jesse Helms
**What They Want You to Forget:** Jesse Helms

### *Oklahoma (OH-KLA-HOMƐ-A or O.K.!L-A-H-O-M-A)*

**Nickname:** Sooner State
**Capital City:** Oklahoma City
**State Motto:** *Labor omnia vincit* (Labor conquers all things)
**State Flower:** Mistletoe
**State Bird:** Scissor-tailed flycatcher
**State Tree:** Redbud
**State Song:** "Oklahoma"
**Famous Natives:** Garth Brooks, Woody Guthrie, Mickey Mantle, Reba McEntire, Daniel Patrick Moynihan, Brad Pitt, Tony Randall
**What They Want You to Remember:** They gave us Brad Pitt.
**What They Want You to Forget:** He's married.

### *South Carolina (SOWTH CA-LIN-UH)*

**Nickname:** Palmetto State
**Capital City:** Columbia
**State Mottoes:** *Animis opibusque parati; Dum spiro spero* (Prepared in mind and resources; While I breathe, I hope)
**State Flower:** Carolina yellow jessamine
**State Bird:** Carolina wren
**State Tree:** Palmetto tree
**State Song:** "Carolina"
**Famous Natives:** Chubby Checker, Joe Frazier, Dizzy Gillespie, Andrew Jackson, Jesse Jackson, Strom Thurmond, Vanna White
**What They Want You to Remember:** Their manners
**What They Want You to Forget:** Your plans for Myrtle Beach next summer

### *Tennessee (TIN-UH-SEE)*

**Nickname:** Volunteer State
**Capital City:** Nashville
**State Motto:** Agriculture and Commerce
**State Flower:** Iris
**State Bird:** Mockingbird
**State Tree:** Tulip poplar
**State Songs:** "The Tennessee Waltz"; "My Homeland, Tennessee"; "Tennessee"; "When It's Iris Time in Tennessee"; "My Tennessee"; "Rocky Top"
**Famous Natives:** Aretha Franklin, Morgan Freeman, Dolly Parton, Minnie Pearl, Cybill Shepherd, Dinah Shore, Tina Turner
**What They Want You to Remember:** Vols Football and the lyrics to "Rocky Top" or "Grand Ole Opry"
**What They Want You to Forget:** Al Gore

### *Texas (TEX-IZ)*

**Nickname:** Lone Star State
**Capital City:** Austin
**State Motto:** Friendship
**State Flower:** Bluebonnet
**State Bird:** Mockingbird
**State Tree:** Pecan
**State Song:** "Texas, Our Texas"
**Famous Natives:** Joan Crawford, Dwight D. Eisenhower, Ben Hogan, Buddy Holly, Lyndon B. Johnson, Janis Joplin, Willie Nelson, Sandra Day O'Connor, Dan Rather
**What They Want You to Remember:** The Alamo
**What They Want You to Forget:** The Branch Davidians and Waco

## *Virginia (VUR-GIN-YUH)*

**Nickname:** The Old Dominion; Mother of Presidents
**Capital City:** Richmond
**State Motto:** *Sic semper tyrannis* (Thus always to tyrants)
**State Flower:** American dogwood
**State Bird:** Cardinal
**State Tree:** Dogwood
**State Song:** "Carry Me Back to Old Virginia"
**Famous Natives:** Arthur Ashe, Pearl Bailey, Warren Beatty, Ella Fitzgerald, Thomas Jefferson, Robert E. Lee, Shirley MacLaine, James Madison, James Monroe, George Washington, Woodrow Wilson, et al. (total of eight presidents, but who's counting?)
**What They Want You to Remember:** They gave us eight presidents, and northern Virginia is different from the rest of Virginia.
**What They Want You to Forget:** They don't have any professional sports teams.

### *Washington, D.C. (WARSH-ing-ton, Hun)*

**Nickname:** DC
**State Motto:** *Justita Omnibus* (Justice to all) (oh, yeah, that's the ticket)
**State Flower:** American Beauty rose
**State Bird:** Wood thrush
**State Tree:** Scarlet oak
**State Song:** "The Star-Spangled Banner"
**Famous Natives:** Duke Ellington, John F. Kennedy, Jr., Samuel L. Jackson, Miss Manners (Judith Martin)
**What They Want You to Remember:** Your campaign contributions
**What They Want You to Forget:** Their traffic jams

### *West Virginia (WES VUR-GIN-YUH)*

**Nickname:** Mountain State
**Capital City:** Charleston
**State Motto:** *Montani semper liberi.* (Mountaineers are always free.)
**State Flower:** Rhododendron
**State Bird:** Cardinal
**State Tree:** Sugar maple
**State Song:** "West Virginia, My Home Sweet Home"; "The West Virginia Hills"; "This Is My West Virginia"
**Famous Natives:** George Brett, Pearl S. Buck, Thomas Stonewall Jackson, Don Knotts, Peter Marshall, Mary Lou Retton
**What They Want You to Remember:** The Greenbrier
**What They Want You to Forget:** Strip mining coal ("Ain't No Mountain High Enough")

## *A League of Its Own*

### South of the Border

South of the Border may not be your final destination, but I defy you to be able to drive by it on I-95 without doing a beeline off the exit. Roller coasters, fireworks, restaurants, campsites, miniature golf courses, cheap motels, souvenir shops, $99 wedding packages, and tacky chic may not be your idea of a family vacation, but it sure beats the average rest stop. Don't worry. You can't miss it. The billboard assault on unsuspecting motorists begins in earnest about 200 miles in either direction from S.O.B. (the South Carolina state line) with signs that make up in quantity what they lack in clarity:

| | |
|---|---|
| Fill Yo' Trunque with Pedro's Junque | 67 miles |
| Making Whoopie | 64 miles |
| Pet Stop | 60 miles |
| If you can't come, write P.O. Box 1328 | 32 miles |
| Roads Scholar (all the letters are upside down) | 21 miles |
| Hats Around the World | 16 miles |
| Your Final Answer | 11 miles |
| Shalom | 9 miles |
| Club Mex | 8 miles |
| You never sausage a place | 3 miles |
| You're always a wiener at Pedro's | 2 miles |

At the end of the long horseshoe exit for S.O.B. that seems to go on for at least three miles, you will enter Mecca: a cross between the neon glitz of a Las Vegas strip or, for East Coasters, the honky-tonk, carnival atmosphere of the Wildwood, New Jersey, boardwalk. Pedro, a mustachioed statue in a sombrero who stands almost 100 feet tall, will be there to greet you. Pedro has a way of compelling just about anyone from the highway—from the bon vivant stepping out of his Lamborghini, to the big-haired, tattooed babe hopping off her Harley, to the family of seven pitching a tent. But they all leave with something in common—a tacky souvenir with the S.O.B. logo.

**Yankee Do! Buy one of Pedro's industrial-size fly swatters.**

## Your Pocket Guide to the Civil War

Naturally, there's more to the South than flora and fauna and famous places and faces. There's that Civil War. Any Yankee who hasn't thought about it since his fifth-grade history test is in for a rude awakening. In the South, the Civil War still falls under current events. You'll need to know your way around the major battlefields to hold your own at cocktail parties. Civil War buffs may not require CliffsNotes, but this is for the rest of us.

### Ten Southern Names for the Civil War

1. The War of Northern Aggression
2. The War of the Rebellion
3. The War to Keep the South
4. The War Between the States
5. The Yankee Invasion
6. The Lost Cause
7. The Uncivil War
8. The Late Unpleasantness
9. Mr. Lincoln's War
10. The War

## "Must-See Battlefields"

| Dates | Name of Battle | Place of Battle | Significance of Battle | Result of Battle |
|---|---|---|---|---|
| Apr. 12–14, 1861 | Fort Sumter | Charleston, SC | First engagement of the Civil War | Confederate victory |
| July 21, 1861 | Manassas (a.k.a. Bull Run) | Manassas, VA | First Manassas: Confederate and Union armies met for the first time, and Union hopes for a short and bloodless war were dashed when 4,700 lay dead at the end of the day. | Confederate victory |
| Feb. 13–16, 1862 | Fort Donelson | Dover, TN | Buckner gave his unconditional surrender to Grant. | Union victory |
| Mar. 6–8, 1862 | Pea Ridge | Pea Ridge, AR | Fight to keep Missouri under Union control. The park includes a segment of the Trail of Tears. | Union victory |
| Apr. 16–17, 1862 | Shiloh | Shiloh, TN | Both sides suffered heavy losses; 24,000 casualties. | Union victory |
| Aug. 28–30, 1862 | Second Manassas | | Decisive battle of the Northern Virginia campaign | Confederate victory |
| Sept. 16–18, 1862 | Antietam | Sharpsburg, MD | Marks the end of Lee's first invasion of the North; 23,000 casualties. Led to Lincoln's issuance of Emancipation Proclamation | Inconclusive; strategic Union victory |
| Dec. 11–15, 1862 | Fredericksburg and Spotsylvania | Fredericksburg, VA | Siege of Richmond, 85,000 wounded, 18,000 killed | Confederate victory |
| Dec. 31, 1862– Jan. 2, 1863 | Stones River | Murfreesboro, TN | Union takes control of middle Tennessee. Boost to the Union after loss at Fredericksburg | Union victory |

*(continued on next page)*

| Dates | Name of Battle | Place of Battle | Significance of Battle | Result of Battle |
|---|---|---|---|---|
| May 18–July 4, 1863 | Vicksburg | Vicksburg, MS | Union wins control of Mississippi River; start of Sherman's March to the Sea | Union victory |
| July 1–3, 1863 | Gettysburg | Gettysburg, PA | Largest, bloodiest Civil War battle; major turning point; single largest loss of American lives in battle, 51,000 killed; where Lincoln delivered the Gettysburg Address | Union victory |
| Apr. 2, 1865 | Petersburg | Petersburg, VA | Grant's capture of Petersburg led to the fall of Richmond, the capital of the Confederacy. | Union victory |
| Apr. 19, 1865 | Appomattox | Appomattox, VA | Lee surrendered to Grant. | Union victory |

**"In Their Own Words"** (a message to Yankees from the Southern Tourism Bureau courtesy the Internet)

*"Don't laugh at our Civil War monuments. If Lee had listened to Longstreet and flanked Meade at Gettysburg instead of sending Pickett up the middle, you'd be paying taxes to Richmond instead of Washington. If you visit Stone Mountain and complain about the carving, we'll kick your ass."*

★ ★ ★ ★ ★ ★ ★ ★ ★

## *Know Your Stars and Bars*

The Confederate flag is alive and well in the South. While its losses on the PC battlefield have led to many casualties (the flag is being removed from Southern town squares one by one), the rebel spirit hasn't flagged. You still regularly see the Confederate flag on bumper stickers and truckers' hats as well as flying from private homes. But contrary to popular opinion, that flag you're seeing is not the Stars and Bars.

**The Stars and Bars**

**The Battle Flag**

The Stars and Bars was the first official flag of the Confederacy, but it was replaced because it was too similar to the Stars and Stripes flag of the Union and resulted in confusion on the battlefield. Its seven stars represent the original Confederate states: South Carolina, Mississippi, Florida, Alabama, Georgia, Louisiana, and Texas.

The Stars and Bars was replaced by the better-known Battle Flag, also known as the Southern Cross. Its thirteen stars represent the original Confederate states plus the last four to secede from the Union: Virginia, Arkansas, Tennessee, and North Carolina. The Battle flag also includes a star for Kentucky and one for Missouri, though their attempts to secede from the Union failed.

**Yankee Don't! Don't wear your "Sock it to me in Alabama" T-shirt to the history museum and pick up the china cups from the Civil War to admire them at closer range. Oh, noooooo, Mr. Bill . . .**

# SCOUT'S HONOR

***With all due respect to*** the Boy Scouts of America, I took the liberty of reworking their merit program to give it something with a little more, well, merit. Come on. If you can earn a medal for helping an old lady cross the street, isn't it high time we reward people who make it across the Mason-Dixon?

## *"Moving and Shaking" Merit Program*

### "Keep the Faith" Badge

Are you there, God? It's me, Alice. If you're Baptist, your prayers will be answered. Jewish? Catholic? Lutheran? Muslim? See your airline for the place of worship nearest you. It's not that Southerners don't accept the religions of their new neighbors. It's just that they don't understand them. They'll sell Chanukah candles in July, for instance. Since Southerners are new to God's chosen people (they only know them from the Bible), Jews may find that shopping for Passover supplies is a bit of an odyssey. Try looking for the "matzo crackers" (*sic*) in a January end-of-aisle display, or check the International Foods section (three shelves) for kosher supplies.

**Yankee Do! Buy your Chanukah candles in July and freeze them! They will only be offered once a year, so get them while you can.**

The road less traveled isn't for everyone, so you may want to think about assimilating. If you've ever considered changing religions, the Baptists have a lot going for them—not the least of which are their church suppers.

Whatever you do, take advantage of your day of rest. You'll be praying for mercy when it's time to get back to business.

### "I Found a Doc" Badge

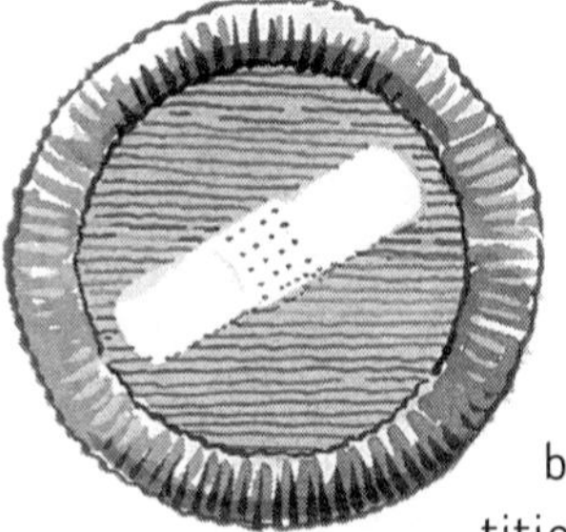

Looking for a top doc? Look no further. Unless, that is, you want to get in to see one. You'll hear "We're not accepting new patients" as much as you'll hear "Your insurance didn't cover that." To earn your "I Found a Doc" badge, all you have to do is find a general practitioner and a dentist taking new patients. Tip: Don't wait till you're in pain. Yankee tears don't open doors down here. And get in the swing of processing your own insurance claims. Receptionists are way too busy turning away new patients to have time to do *your* paperwork.

**Yankee Do! Fake a Southern accent when calling to get an appointment with Dr. B. Happy, or take advantage of the IRS tax break and fly home to see a doc you know and love.**

### "Beauty and the Beast" Badge

Wait till you see your new Southern 'do. Think bouffant (for men and women). Need your hair colored? Two choices. White for men, yellow for women. To earn your "Beauty and the Beast" badge, find a stylist (his or her) who can cut your hair in a coiffure close enough to your old look that you'd be recognized in before and after photos.

**Yankee Do! Bring a bandanna.**

### "Bug Off" Badge

Get ready to cohabitate with snakes, lizards, and toads, oh my! They're like the bugs you know, only bigger. Apparently, the roaches aren't eating Lean Cuisine. They're 3x their typical size. And while the ants come in every color, don't be fooled by their good looks—they bite. Centipedes must be in the witness protection program. They go by the name of rolypoly here.

To earn your "Bug Off" badge, you must: (1) learn to see the beauty in the little giraffe-colored snake perched on your porch rocking chair; (2) enjoy the earnestness of the tree frogs using their suction cup feet to stare into your kitchen window; and (3) stop fainting in the tub when you lather up and see a palmetto bug on the showerhead. Learn to embrace nature, and stop being such a wimp. Sure, the dragonflies dive-bomb you every time you go out for the mail; just wear a mosquito net like Katharine Hepburn in *African Queen.*

**Yankee Don't! Don't "go to pieces" if you see a "pantry pest." It's easier and cheaper to just move again.**

### "Driving Miss Daisy" Badge

All you have to do to earn this badge is read your new driver's manual and survive one tool around the neighborhood—beware of center turning lanes!

## *The Southern Two-Second Rule*

**(DMV Driver's Handbook, North Carolina)**

The "two-second" rule says that you should allow two seconds between the time the vehicle ahead of you passes a given point and the time your vehicle reaches the same point.

## *The Yankee Two-Second Rule*

**(No Books Required, Road-Schooled)**

The "two-second" rule says that if the person in front of you takes more than two seconds to respond to the light changing green, you must lay your entire body on the horn.

**"In Their Own Words"** (my Southern driving instructor)

*"You see, traffic used to be paced and measured. And then, may I say, we had a tremendous influx of more aggressive drivers. (Read: Yankees) It's embarrassing, but now you have to strap on a bayonet. The custom in the South was that if you had a funeral procession coming toward you, to show respect you would get off the road and let them bury their dead. In '85, you started to see cars that would keep going. No courtesy. No compassion. A realtor told me IBM started it. People from the North and West moving in and snapping up those big houses."*

**Yankee Do! If you see a hearse on the other side of the road, don't forget to express your condolences. Pull over to the side of the road. (No, Weeping Zones are not marked, so be prepared to cause a six-car pile-up.) If you have a casserole on you, pass it out the window.**

***These authentic bumper stickers represent the Southern hospitality we hear so much about.***

- I'd Rather Be Shooting Yankees
- Happiness Is a North Bound Yankee
- If You ❤ New York, Take I-95 North
- Teach a Yankee to Drive. Point His Car North
- I Don't Care How You Did It Up North
- God, Guns & Guts. Keep America Free.
- American By Birth, Southern By the Grace of God
- I ❤ G.R.I.T.S. Girls Raised In The South
- It's Too Bad Everybody Couldn't Be Southern
- Confederate By Choice, Union By Force

**Taxi!**

The South is home to approximately 100 million people. They share about six taxis, so you may want to wet your whistle before attempting to hail a cab. Need to get to the airport on time? Consider springing for a limousine. Just remember: Even the limo drivers are laid-back in the South. They don't make catching your plane a priority.

### "School Days" Badge

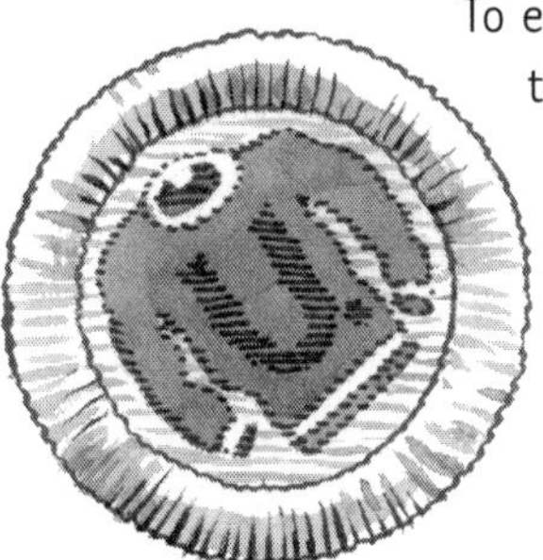

To earn your "School Days" badge, you don't have to complete a four-year program, all you have to do is give it the old college try—and get accepted to a Southern university, including, but not limited to the following schools.

★ ★ ★ ★ ★ ★ ★ ★ ★

| School | Nicknames |
|---|---|
| University of Alabama | 'Bama; Crimson Tide |
| University of Arkansas | Razorbacks |
| University of Delaware | Blue Hens |
| Florida State University | Seminoles |
| Georgetown University | Hoyas |
| University of Georgia | Bulldawgs |
| University of Kentucky | Wildcats |
| Louisiana State University | Tigers |
| University of Maryland | Terps |
| University of Mississippi | Ole Miss |
| University of North Carolina | Tar Heels |
| University of Oklahoma | Sooners |
| University of South Carolina | Gamecocks |
| University of Tennessee | Volunteers |
| University of Texas | Longhorns |
| University of Virginia | Wahoos, Cavaliers |
| West Virginia University | Mountaineers |

| *How to Get In* | *Why to Get In* |
|---|---|
| weigh 305 lbs., bench press 450, and run a 4.8 40-yard dash | the homecoming pep rally; the Crimson Tide has won more national championships than any other college football team |
| read at a sixth-grade level | great frat parties |
| live in Delaware | Kegstands and Cluck-U |
| do the chop to distract the dean from your SATs | consistently ranked among the top party schools in the nation/to get thrown in the fountain on your birthday |
| with a note from the Pope | to decide your future: the Senate or the House |
| have Sonny Seiler tip the scales of justice in your favor | to own a bulldog named Uga |
| get recruited by the Louisville Cardinals | to see a basketball game from the Eruption Zone |
| tell them Shaq sent you | to get sloppy |
| live outside the Beltway | to stay outside the Beltway |
| dress for success | to *grove* in the height of fashion (According to the fashionistas at *Women's Wear Daily,* Ole Miss is one of the top ten most fashionable schools in the country.) |
| 6'8" with a 25-foot jump shot | Easy A's—according to lore, you just drink out of the Old Well on the first day of school |
| get recruited by Texas | to play pickleball |
| Rush Week | to Delta Delta Delta your way to the top |
| wear orange (even your prison jumpsuit) | number one party school nod from the *Princeton Review,* and the resulting "crackdown" didn't take |
| ride a Longhorn to the interview | clubbing on Sixth Street |
| perfect score on the SATs | speakers like the Dalai Lama |
| Be a Hatfield, or is it a McCoy? | Up All Night program, and you can get credit for fishing |

## *Who Am I?*

To complete the merit program, you'll need a title badge. You're either an "Honorary Southerner" or a "Damn Yankee." You can't play for both teams. If you responded well to college hazings and have any experience in sororities, then "Honorary Southerner" a.k.a. "Reformed Yankee" is likely the best route for you. Sure, you'll have to turn your back on the person formerly known as you, but so what. *They like you. They like you.* If, on the other hand, your favorite song is Frank Sinatra's "My Way," you're destined to be a Damn Yankee. The choice is yours.

**"Honorary Southerner" Badge**

To become a "best friend," a.k.a. "Honorary Southerner" or "Reformed Yankee," you've got to be willing to pay the dues:

- Eat chitlins (hog intestines)
- Eat grits
- Drink sweet tea without going into sugar shock
- Develop a fake accent (practice starts with "hi, y'all" and goes South from there)
- Pass propaganda to your friends back home—positioning the South as the only place to be ("Twenty below there? Really? I have my bathing suit on here.")

★ ★ ★ ★ ★ ★ ★ ★ ★

**"Damn Yankee" Badge**

If you're unwilling to lose your nasal accent and *Stepford* into your kinder, gentler Southern skin, you will fall into disrepute and be labeled as "Yankee," "Damn Yankee," or "G.D. Yankee." For a full explanation, see any Southerner with a bag of jokes. They're sure to have one that goes something like this: A Yankee moves south for a while but then heads back north. A Damn Yankee moves south and stays. A G.D. Yankee moves south for good but never stops whining about the good ole days up north.

## *Minority Report*

Study up before you get here! A Hispanic newcomer will instantly become his neighbor's encyclopedia for all things Latino. Even if you're third generation and your family has been living in Arizona since 1901, Southerners will pepper you with questions about your culture. Same thing if you're Jewish. They will ask you hundreds of questions about your faith, history, and culture. Minorities in the South are constantly on the Internet looking up things for the company picnic just to keep up with demand. Inquiring minds want to know! Minorities often claim they get more in touch with their heritage when they move here. Once they get used to being an ambassador for their people, they kind of like it.

Yankee African Americans are relieved to find that, contrary to popular belief, it's not still the 1960s down here. There are plenty of great places to live that are not homogenous or exclusive. Rural pockets may be integrating more slowly, and we still pale in comparison to the diversity of the big cities, but we've come a long way, baby.

## *Got Mail?*

It's not that you won't hear about what's going on with the rest of the world, it's just that it may take a while. Looking for your *Time* magazine on Monday? Not going to happen. Down here, everything is a bit delayed. We start the news week on Tuesday or Wednesday. "What's your hurry?" defines Southern Standard Time, and there's nothing in the mail that can't wait until tomorrow. This is not to say Southerners don't take their mailboxes seriously. Mailboxes are yet another way to express your personal decorating style as well as gardening finesse. Climbing vines around the post? Seasonal annuals at the base?

## *Hold the Pepperoni*

The good news is that most Yankees seem to somehow find a doctor who can ease the pain, a dentist to whom they can show their bite, a stylist who makes Joe's $2 cuts look good, a place to mind their p's&q's, and a God who will listen when they don't. But one thing they never find: pizza like they had back home. New York style? Fuggedaboutit! Chicago deep-dish? You've got a better chance of Michael Jordan delivering it to you.

★ ★ ★ ★ ★ ★ ★ ★ ★

### How to Know If You're Fitting In

1. Your neighbors cancel the bus ticket they bought to send you back where ya came from.
2. They ask you to play General Robert E. Lee at the Civil War reenactment party.
3. Your Labrador retriever gets into a top obedience school.
4. People keep admiring your lovely carpetbag, ahh . . . I mean carpet.
5. You're accepted at Alcoholics Anonymous.

★ ★ ★ ★ ★ ★ ★ ★ ★

### How to Know That You're Not

1. On Halloween, the neighborhood kids dress up as you and your husband.
2. The trained parrot next door imitates your accent.
3. Your neighbor sends a video of your visiting relatives to *America's Funniest Home Videos.*
4. You're invited next door for chitlins, and they ask you to clean the hogs.
5. They ask you to carry the French flag at a rally to celebrate our troops.

CHAPTER 8

# *Sports Illustrated* Meets *Southern Living*, or My Compliments to the Ref

***Calling all sports fans!*** Who needs the heartbreak of a big-city team when you can have a team that is always in the Final Four? Forget "How 'bout them Eagles?" How 'bout them Blue Devils? How 'bout them Wildcats? In lieu of big-city pro teams, college sports are the teams to beat in the South. Baseball fans, don't look so forlorn. How 'bout them minors? Need a little more action than that? Gentlemen, start your engines. Welcome to the home of NASCAR! And remember, it's never too late to take up golf.

## College Basketball

There are only two conferences we care about in the South: the ACC and the SEC. And if you weren't a follower before, you had best get in the game. Southerners are college hoops fanatics, and encouraged from an early age to strategically secure friendships (read: seats) in other ACC/SEC cities. Business comes to a standstill during March Madness. And even the God-fearing throw caution to the wind and play in the NCAA pools. WWJP? Whom Would Jesus Pick?

### The ACC

| School | Nickname | Colors to Paint Your Face | Team to Hate |
|---|---|---|---|
| Clemson | Tigers | Orange and Purple | UNC |
| Duke | Blue Devils | Blue and White | UNC |
| Florida State | FSU Seminoles | Garnet (red) and Gold | Duke |
| Georgia Tech | Yellow Jackets | White and Gold | Duke |
| Maryland | Terps (Terrapins) | Red, White, Black, and Gold | Virginia |
| Miami | Hurricanes | Orange, Green, and White | Florida State |
| North Carolina | Tar Heels | Light Blue and White | Duke |
| NC State | Wolfpack | Red and White | UNC |
| Virginia | Cavaliers | Navy Blue and Orange | Duke |
| Virginia Tech | Hokies | Maroon and Burnt Orange | Miami |
| Wake Forest | Demon Deacons | Black and Gold | Everybody |

## The SEC

| School | Nickname | Colors to Paint Your Face | Team to Hate |
|---|---|---|---|
| Alabama | Crimson Tide | Crimson (red) and White | Florida |
| Arkansas | Razorbacks | Cardinal (red) and White | Florida |
| Auburn | Tigers | Navy Blue and Burnt Orange | Florida |
| Florida | Gators | Orange and Blue | Everybody |
| Georgia | Bulldogs (Dawgs) | Red and Black | Florida |
| Kentucky | Wildcats | Blue and White | Florida |
| Louisiana State | Tigers | Purple and Gold | Florida |
| Mississippi (Ole Miss) | Rebels | Navy Blue and Cardinal Red | Florida |
| Mississippi State | Bulldogs | Maroon and White | Florida |
| South Carolina | Gamecocks | Garnet (red) and Black | Florida |
| Tennessee | Volunteers or Vols | Orange and White | Florida |
| Vanderbilt | Commodores or Vandy | Black and Gold | Florida |

★ ★ ★ ★ ★ ★ ★ ★ ★

## *Are You Ready For Some Football?!*

Naturally, the ACC and SEC schools mentioned above aren't all basketball all the time. These schools also have football programs. The problem is—how to put this kindly? They didn't all make the cut. Of course, you can support any team you like, no matter how big or small, how good or bad. But for the purposes of this chapter, we're going to concentrate on teams that play in what we'll call the *SLC—Southern Living* Conference.

Now, before you start mocking a region that turns to *Southern Living* for its football issue (gotta love the Halftime Hospitality Recipes) and whose heart beats to the rhythm of a marching band, you have to consider all of the facts. College football teams in the South are playing in front of capacity crowds that equal the rabid fandom of NFL teams in the top cities in the country. Alabama's Crimson Tide plays in front of sold-out crowds of 84,000, compared to, say, the Philadelphia Eagles, who play to the tune of 66,000. And you don't ever want to tell a Southern tailgater that his deviled eggs aren't the meanest ones you've ever eaten. You know what they say; if you can't beat 'em, join 'em!

## *The Menu for the Southern Tailgate*

- **Deviled Eggs—Resplendent in paprika and parsley**

Southerners bring these to the game with a straight face. I kid you not, real men bring deviled eggs, and Gentlemen (to reflect proper Southern raising) bring deviled eggs with a small sprig of parsley per egg to show their refinement.

- **Country ham biscuits**

The biscuits are arranged in a shoebox between layers of waxed paper. We're talking hand-rolled biscuits, as any Southerner knows that the Pillsbury Dough Boy would bring bad luck to his team and shame on his mama. The ham must be well-cured country ham (more salt than ham is ideal) and cannot under any circumstances be ham from a "deli."

- **Pimiento cheese sandwiches**

- **A Jell-O salad**

A salad only Bill Cosby could love

- **Bloody Marys (from a secret family recipe)**

- **Cheese straws (they may look like cookies, but they taste like straw) and boiled peanuts**

## Cheers and Jeers

**Cheers:** Your Bloody's all right!
**Jeers!** Ho!Ho! Hey! Hey! Your deviled eggs are bland today!

## Game Day Traditions—Pump It Up, Southern Style

- **Clemson:** The Tigers know how to make an entrance. Rubbing the rock and running down the hill has been described as the most exciting 25 seconds of college football.
- **Florida State:** The Seminoles start each game with Chief Osceola galloping onto the field on his handsome horse, Renegade, and toting a fire-blazing spear. The chief hurls the flaming spear into the Seminoles' logo on the 50-yard line, igniting a furious enthusiasm in 85,000 fans. They show their appreciation by doing the tomahawk chop and singing the war chant, music to the garnet-and-gold ears of a 'Nole fan.
- **Louisiana State University:** Mike, the full-grown Bengal tiger, is loaded into the LSU cage (cheerleaders ride on top), and he's wheeled into the stadium.
- **Mississippi State:** Bulldogs ring cowbells and shout "Hoddy Totty." (The fact that cowbells and Confederate battle flags have been banned from athletic contests notwithstanding. See no evil, hear no evil.)
- **Ole Miss:** A firm believer in "groving"—extensive mingling during tailgate parties. (The Grove is 10 acres of grassy ground and oak trees in the center of campus.)
- **Oklahoma:** A runaway chuck wagon bursts out of the tunnel before each Sooners game.

- **Tennessee:** Smoky, the blue tick coonhound, leads the Volunteers through the big "T" formed by the Southland Band, and then he stays on the sidelines for inspiration. Smoky's prerecorded growl is played over the public address system whenever the Vols score.
- **University of Virginia:** UVA has a tradition of pleading the "fourth year fifth." (Founder Thomas Jefferson didn't believe in the titles freshman, sophomore, etc.; ergo, first-years through fourth-years.) Fourth-years drink a fifth of bourbon at the last football game of the season. Dressing up for games is also a tradition—a throwback to the days when UVA was all male, and the game was the place to meet girls.

### *Some Chants to Get You Going*

| | |
|---|---|
| Alabama | Roll Tide Roll! |
| Arkansas | Woo Pigs Sooiee! Woo Pigs Sooiee! Woo Pigs Sooiee! Razorbacks! |
| Auburn | Hey! War Eagle |
| Clemson | Roar (canon fires) Tigers! |
| Florida | (to the tune of *Jaws* theme) Go Gators! |
| Georgia | Go Dawgs! Sic 'em! Woof!Woof!Woof! |
| Georgia Tech | Go Jackets! Sting 'em! Bzzzzzzzzzzzz |
| NC State | Go Pack! |
| Oklahoma | Sooner born and Sooner bred; when I die, I'll be Sooner dead. |
| South Carolina | Go Cocks! Fight! Win! |
| Texas A&M | Ay, Ay, Ay, Whoop! |
| Vanderbilt | Go 'Dores! |
| Virginia | U . . . V . . . A. UVA, Go Hoos go! |

## *Fore!*

**GOLF: It's Not Just a Game. It's a Way of Life.**

### The Legend In His Own Mind

**Handicap:** 12 to 15

**Constant Replay (the instant replay the golfer always talks about):** Eagle chip at Pinehurst (11 years ago)

**Favorite Golf Metaphor:** It's a slice if it goes right. It's a hook if it goes left. It's a miracle if it goes straight. He says, "That's a chip shot" for anything in life (on course or off course) that's easy.

**What's in My Bag?** The latest and greatest oversized driver they make, ball retriever, copper wristband, sandpaper, pliers and lead tape "just like (*name of his golf hero here*)," Nabs, and Advil

---

### The All-Around Athlete

**Handicap:** 8 to 9

**Constant Replay (the instant replay the golfer always talks about):** Beat the pro at Calloway Gardens

**Favorite Golf Metaphor:** "Tough putt" for any life challenge

**What's in My Bag?** Three wedges, Gatorade, cartoon head covers: Pluto for his driver, Bugs Bunny for three wood, and Tweetie Bird for five wood

**Handicap:** Like her age, it's on a need-to-know basis

**Constant Replay (the instant replay the golfer always talks about):** Golf skirt split at Hilton Head the day she met the governor's wife at the ninth hole

**Favorite Golf Metaphor:** Stroke it smooth, or I may not play well, but I look good.

**What's in My Bag?** Four woods, safety pins (for future skirt mishaps), lipstick, plastic thermos of sweet tea, pastel headcovers with pom-poms, a compact, breath mints, and a battery-operated handheld fan

---

**Handicap:** Gets "doctored" regularly (20 to 22)

**Constant Replay (the instant replay the golfer always talks about):** Hole in one at North Ridge in '71 (only witness is dead)

**Favorite Golf Metaphor:** I must have hit that one on the screws, boys.

**What's in My Bag?** Bananas, Centrum Silver, change of socks (feet sweat), liniment, twenty golf balls, milk of magnesia, Depends, wooden woods

**Handicap:** 6
**Constant Replay (the instant replay the golfer always talks about):** Won the longest drive at the company picnic; didn't play from the ladies' tees
**Favorite Golf Metaphor:** Tee to the greens
**What's in My Bag?** Men's driver, 60-degree wedge, change of shirt, yardage scope, Red Bull

---

**Handicap:** His mother, bless her heart
**Constant Replay (the instant replay the golfer always talks about):** "Homerun" on the sixteenth after dark
**Favorite Golf Metaphor:** We like to swing.
**What's in My Bag?** Matching Pings for him and her, sun block

## The Redneck

**Handicap:** Uh, you do the math (20 to 28?)

**Constant Replay (the instant replay the golfer always talks about):** Got hammered and drove the cart into the pond at "The Witch" in Myrtle Beach. Drank a beer a hole!

**Favorite Golf Metaphor:** Drive for show, putt for dough, or Shot a Birdie (with a gun)

**What's in My Bag?** Mixed set of knockoff clubs ("vintage"), Pepto-Bismol, Jim Beam, six-pack, bag o' chaw, Slim Jims, empty hot dog wrappers and score cards from every round ever played, empty golf ball sleeves, Tampa Nugget cigars.

The Redneck can't always get out to the Club, so he'll make a do-it-yourself course at home: shaved patch of lawn, fishing pole for the pin (the pennant is secured with duct tape), a Dixie tumbler for the cup, and two burn piles for sand traps.

## *The Who's Who of Some of the South's Premier Golf Courses*

**For a Southern course with a little more cachet . . .**

| The Course | Location |
| --- | --- |
| Shoal Creek Golf Club | Birmingham, Alabama |
| Pinnacle Country Club | Rogers, Arkansas |
| Wilmington Country Club (South Course) | Wilmington, Delaware |
| Doral Golf Resort & Spa (Blue Monster) | Miami, Florida |
| Augusta National Golf Club | Augusta, Georgia |
| Valhalla Golf Course | Louisville, Kentucky |
| English Turn Golf & Country Club | New Orleans, Louisiana |
| Congressional Country Club (Blue) | Bethesda, Maryland |
| Old Waverly Golf Club | West Point, Mississippi |
| Pinehurst Resort & Country Club (No. 2) | Pinehurst, North Carolina |
| Southern Hills Country Club | Tulsa, Oklahoma |
| Sea Pines Resort (Harbour Town Golf Links) | Hilton Head, South Carolina |
| The Honors Course | Ooltewah, Tennessee |
| Colonial Country Club | Fort Worth, Texas |
| The Homestead (Cascades) | Hot Springs, Virginia |
| The Greenbrier | White Sulphur Springs, West Virginia |

| Designed By | Signature Hole | Greens Fees* |
|---|---|---|
| Jack Nicklaus | #14, a scenic par 4 | $95 |
| Donald Sechrest | #14, a 596-yard par 5 | $120 |
| Robert Trent Jones | #17, a 210-yard par 3 over water | $110 |
| Dick Wilson and Bob VonHagge | #18, a 460-yard dogleg left par 4 | $275 |
| Bobby Jones & Alister Mackenzie | #11, 12 & 13 "Amen Corner" | KEEP OFF THE GRASS |
| Jack Nicklaus | #13, a 350-yard par 4 | $85 |
| Jack Nicklaus | #18, a 471-yard par 4, is ranked as one of the three hardest holes on the PGA tour | $155 |
| Devereux Emmet | #17, a 466-yard par 4 | $165 |
| Bob Cupp & Jerry Pate | #16, a 422-yard par 4 | $124 weekends, $94 weekdays |
| Donald Ross | #5, one of the most difficult par 4's ever—just ask the '99 U.S. Open players | $335 |
| Perry Maxwell | #12, Arnold Palmer's favorite par 4 | $100 |
| Pete Dye and Jack Nicklaus | #18, a 452-yard par 4 | $250 |
| Pete Dye | #15, a 445-yard par 4 with a peninsula space | $85 |
| Perry Maxwell | #5, a 470-yard par 4 | $200 |
| William S. Flynn | a 210-yard par 3 named "Carry On" | $205 |
| Jack Nicklaus | #2, with trees to the left and a pond to the right, the course's toughest tee shot | $180 |

*Fore! Restrictive guest policies may apply, and greens fees are subject to change.

## *NASCAR*
## *(National Association for Stock Car Auto Racing)*

Baseball may be as American as apple pie, but NASCAR is as Southern as pecan pie. Dirt track racing got its *official* start in Daytona in 1948, and it got its unofficial start from Southern moonshiners after World War II. They made their own booze to avoid paying taxes and raced around the farmlands at breakneck speeds to make sure all their customers could celebrate happy hour. "Now, that looks like fun." And a sport is born.

Despite its humble origins, NASCAR has blossomed from a regional sport into a national phenomenon and the country's top-grossing sport. Thanks to its expansion across the country, TV coverage, and beauty makeovers for its fans and tracks (VIP boxes put the posh in pits), NASCAR has made it to the big time. But there's no place like home. Almost all of the top racers hail from the South. North Carolina is home to virtually all of the top teams.

The time is now to get in touch with your inner stock car racer. Chew some tobacco while you chew on some facts:

★ ★ ★ ★ ★ ★ ★ ★ ★

## *A Beginner's-Only Course for NASCAR*

### The Team

The driver, the pit crew, including the over-the-wall crew (if you can change four tires, refuel a car, and fix a rearview mirror in under fifteen seconds, we've got the job for you). The number on the crew varies according to team financials, but rich or not, NASCAR only allows seven members of the team to go "over the wall." The lucky seven: the front tire changer, the rear tire changer, the front tire carrier, the rear tire carrier, the jackman, the gas man, and the catch can man. Names are self-explanatory, with the exception of "catch can man"—he's catching overflow gas to avoid fire hazard.

### The Main Events

**The Nextel Cup Series:** (The Winston Cup is so 700 million dollars ago!) The be-all and end-all of racing series. It's making it to the pros, if you will. The best football players in the nation play in the NFL, the best basketball players play in the NBA, and the best stock car racers in the nation race in the Nextel Cup Series.
**The Busch Series:** A feeder series for the Nextel Cup where the semi-pros prep for the pros. Sure, some racers make a life out of it, passing on the pressure of the Nextel Cup, but most of the racers have their sights set for racing to greater heights.
**The Craftsmen Truck Series:** The best of the best for souped-up trucks

### The Point System

The winner of each race pockets 180 points, but the loser doesn't go home empty-handed. The runner-up scores 170, and the points decline in ever decreasing increments down to the last-place finisher, who drives away with 34 points—not bad for just taking the green (showing up). Drivers can win 5 extra points for leading a lap, and there are 5 additional points for the guy who leads the most laps. Points are cumulative over the entire racing season, but the rules have been tweaked to add excitement to the final ten races. The top ten leaders in points earn a berth in the "Chase for the Championship." Points are adjusted so that all qualifying drivers start their sprint to the finish with only 5-point increments dividing them from their closest competitor.

## Track Talk

**Trading paint**—slang term for aggressive driving involving a lot of bumping and rubbing
**Dirty air**—the air used and discarded by the lead car
**Groove**—the best route around the racetrack
**Happy hour**—the last official practice session
**Stickers**—new tires
**Binders**—brakes

## The Flags

**Red:** Stop.
**Green:** Go! Go! Go!
**Yellow:** Caution, slow down.
**Black:** Come into the pit. We've gotta tawk.
**Black with white cross:** For racers who ignore the black flag. It ain't nice to ignore Mother Nature. NASCAR won't score you until you come into the pit and talk to us *now.*
**Blue with yellow stripe:** Check your mirrors—a faster car is coming up behind.
**Yellow with red vertical stripes:** Debris or slippery conditions ahead.
**White:** One lap remaining.
**Checkered:** The event is over, dude.

**Yankee Do! Tired of reading flags? Rent a radio at the race and eavesdrop on the crew. (You'd be surprised what Driver's Ed never taught you.)**

**Yankee Don't! Ladies, it's not mandatory to lift your shirt when your favorite racer drives by, so don't do it just to fit in, do it because you want to.**

If you want to know how important NASCAR is in the South, just ask the politicians who have lost interest in soccer moms and are in heavy pursuit of "NASCAR dads."

★ ★ ★ ★ ★ ★ ★ ★ ★

## *Hunting*

Hunting is not only accepted, it's expected. Opening day of hunting season is a high holiday and a perfectly reasonable way to get out of jury duty. You'll actually see deer slung over the hoods of trucks in the high school parking lots. (Show and tell?) What's not to love about a kid who goes hunting before school, bags a big deer, and calls Daddy when the bell rings to help tackle today's assignment? The last thing I want to do is come between a hunter and his son, so let me just move along here.

Yankee hunters, accustomed to being on the outs up north ("That's so cruel") will now be members of the in-crowd. Those who have come before them rave about the liberal licenses, long seasons, substantially greater bag limits, and spectacular turkey hunting. If it weren't for those dang snakes, it would be a hunter's paradise. Speaking of which, what do you get the hunter who has everything? Membership in one of the $70,000 private hunting clubs!

**Yankee Don't! Hunters who ain't from around here are the only ones who gut their own deer. As every Southern gentleman knows, that's the butcher's job.**

**Yankee Don't! Don't sport a bumper sticker that says "Hunting is Murder" unless you want to be hunted yourself.**

★ ★ ★ ★ ★ ★ ★ ★ ★

## *Gone Fishin'*

In the South, fishing isn't a pastime—it's a priority. A $50,000 home will have a $20,000 boat and a $3,000 pickup truck in the yard. Bait 'n' tackles are easier to find than ATMs, and kids who can't afford the luxury of the corner store raise their own worms to feed their habit. The old cane pole may as well be the symbol of the South, and you don't have to be on the lake to see one. They're all over the road in the summer. Apparently, fishermen are big on carpooling. You'll see a carload of guys and half a dozen 12-foot cane poles sticking out the back window. You'd be hard-pressed to find the Southern guy who doesn't know his way around a murky pond and a five-gallon bucket. What about the Southern women? Just ask grandma. Fishing is for ladies, too.

**Yankee Do! Pack Nabs and Cokes and you'll at least have the Southern fisherman, if not the fish, taking the bait.**

**Yankee Don't! Do not tell a Southern fisherman he is better off with a rod and reel or he is sure to beat you with his cane pole. Literally and figuratively.**

## *Quiz #4 Southern Fried Sports Quiz*

1. **Which of these coach's sentiments was expressed by Bear Bryant:**
   A. 90% of the game is half mental.
   B. I ain't never been nothing but a winner.
   C. We're lost, but we're making good time.
   D. Nobody goes there anymore; it's too crowded.

2. **Why is the Kentucky Derby more prestigious than the Belmont Stakes?**
   A. The women wear prettier hats.
   B. Mint juleps outrank anything New York can shake up.
   C. It's a quarter mile shorter, and horse fans have attention deficit disorder.
   D. It is the first leg of the Triple Crown.

3. **Why do Southerners root for USC?**
   A. They think it stands for University of South Carolina.
   B. They don't.
   C. Southern hospitality.
   D. Because California boys are the cutest boys in the world.

4. **Why do Southern cheerleaders look cuter than their Northern counterparts?**
   A. It's their life's work.
   B. Surveys say men prefer belles.
   C. More role models—more Barbie dolls per capita in the South.
   D. By the age of seventeen they've done everything there is to do in the South.

5. **Why can NASCAR declare a champion with a full month left in the season?**
   A. Because there are *only* fifteen races to go, and everyone's tired of it.
   B. It doesn't end the suspense because the fans can't read the newspaper.
   C. They can't—the new Chase for the Championship keeps you guessing till the last checkered flag.

D. With the point system, it's mathematically impossible to overtake him.

**6. Pound for pound, who has the best college team in the South?**

A. Ole Miss

B. New Miss

C. The Jaguars

D. [Your team here]

**7. Who belongs in the sports motivators' Hall of Fame?**

A. Bear Bryant

B. The Dallas Cowboys cheerleaders

C. Dean Smith

D. All of the above

**8. Where does Bear Bryant sit in heaven?**

A. To the right hand of God

B. With the 'Bama fans

C. Next to Elvis

D. All of the above

**9. What is the most serious psychological illness?**

A. March madness

B. *Monday Night Football* withdrawal

C. Blue Devil Satanism

D. Relational disorder (quarterback is making me crazy)

**10. Which horse has the record at the Kentucky Derby, one of only two horses to ever finish in less than two minutes?**

A. Secretariat

B. Seabiscuit

C. The Horse with no name

D. Monarchos

**Answers: BDBBCDDDDA**

**Unanswered Questions:** How does the mild-mannered tell-it-like-it-isn't South explain their native son, Tell-It-Like-It-Is Howard Cosell?

Chapter 9

# Wedding Belle Blues

***You may not make a love connection*** with a Southerner, but someone will. And you'll be invited to watch. And despite what the blushing brides will have you believe, the average Southern wedding doesn't compare to the love fests back home. Yankees spare no expense on elaborate sit-down dinners, five-piece bands, and fully stocked bars. Baptists don't drink, or at least don't admit to it, so down here, it's sweet tea and cookies at the church social hall, or if they're going all out, hors d'oeuvres with a glass of red or white. Tasteful, sure, but I kind of miss the receptions where everyone drinks their weight in alcohol and dances on the tables until a fight breaks out.

## Southern Wedding Invitation

*Mr. and Mrs. God Fearing*
*request the honor of your presents (no cash)*
*at the marriage of their daughter,*
*Sweet Magnolia,*
*to the poor but honest*
*Jimmy John Upright IV.*
*Crystal, china, and silver preferred.*
*No drinking and dancing.*

## Yankee Wedding Invitation

*Mr. and Mrs. Upton Cumming*
*announce the marriage of their daughter,*
*Cheryl Anne,*
*to New York Jets season ticket holder,*
*Tom Tailgater.*
*The bride has been outfitted with a*
*special pocketbook that holds up to $20,000 in cash.*
*Visa and MasterCard accepted.*

**Yankee Don't! Don't go to a Southern wedding hungry.**

Yankees have come to expect at least a five-course meal (as the guests indulge in the heavy food and drink, the bride has ample time to waltz around to all 400 tables to collect the cash), while Southerners are accustomed to a more casual affair that would suggest that wedding day is no day to worry about what's for dinner.

## *The Wedding Plan*

**Southerners:** Start to finish, including drive time: 3 hours
**Yankees:** Start to finish: 24 hours

## *The Menu*

### *Yankees*

Salad
Surf and Turf
Baked potato
Green vegetables
Dessert (cheesecake or
Baked Alaska)
Coffee
Unlimited alcohol

### *Southerners*

Two cookies
Sweet tea, lemonade (or
punch the same color as
the bridesmaids' dresses)
Unlimited green mints

## Southern Wedding Take 2

Not all Southerners settle for cookies and mints, of course. There are some extravagant ceremonies where dancing and drinking are allowed, the food is plentiful, and every detail of the blessed event has been orchestrated. I have some good news for the Yankees who truly appreciated the dreaded church lady from *Saturday Night Live.* She lives! (Church lady, enter stage right.)

In the South, it's the church lady's job to:

- Keep the high-spirited bride and groom from "cutting up" during wedding planning and the ceremony itself (marriage is serious business).
- Check the guest list and check it twice to find out whose marriage is naught and whose is still nice (second wives, bless their hearts, tend to complicate seating arrangements).
- Make sure the bride's dressing room in the church is up to snuff—Southern brides get dressed at the church, yes, including makeup (it's the maid of honor's role to run back and forth to the bride's home to retrieve everything she forgets).
- Hand signal the organ player when it's time to play "Here Comes the Bride."
- Hand signal the groom when he has his left hand over his right instead of his right over his left (or is it the other way around?) when awaiting his bride-to-be.
- Wave the guests down when the bride's signals for the musician and the groom get crossed, and the guests get up before the she is ready for prime time.

In other words, the church lady will do everything in her power to make sure "her wedding" qualifies as a *Southern Living* wedding.

## *How to Get Your Wedding in Southern Living (the actual application)*

**1. Briefly, how will your wedding positively reflect the South?**

______________________________

______________________________

**2. Unusual musical elements in your wedding (bagpipe, gospel choir, etc.)**

______________________________

______________________________

**3. Creative use of family heirlooms**

______________________________

______________________________

## *Twenty-four-Hour Showers, Roasts, and Toasts*

The Southern bride is showered with love *("bridolized")* from the minute she says "I do." Let's make that "I will." As soon as the engagement is official, the festivities begin. The bride's aunts, girlfriends, and maid of honor all throw different showers: the lingerie shower, the bathroom shower, the stock-the-pantry shower, and the stock-the-bar shower, not to mention the round-the-clock shower (each guest gets a time of day and has to come up with a time-appropriate gift: the "your time is 10 A.M." guest would do herself proud with a coffeepot, for instance). Then there are the non-gift-giving parties where ten to twenty of the bride's parents' closest friends chip in for a restaurant or cater a home affair to *toast* the happy couple. Not to be confused with the rehearsal dinner party, where they *roast* the happy couple. This informal let-down-your-hair night (unless it's an updo, of course) is usually hosted by the groom's family and includes just the wedding party and the couple's immediate families and maybe some out-of-town guests who are close to the couple. The groom's cake (more on that in a minute) is sometimes served at rehearsal dinner rather than the wedding day.

## *Here Comes the Groom*

In the South, it is a tradition to have two wedding cakes. There's the traditional wedding cake (said to be for fertility) and the groom's cake, often chocolate (meant to symbolize a sweet life to come). The groom's cake is all in fun and provides an opportunity to learn a little about the guy: a chocolate and vanilla golf bag for the golfer, a key lime fishing pole for the beau who lives to fish, or a strawberry and vanilla football field for the NC State groom who bleeds red. The groom's cake is a staple at Southern weddings from the church social hall to the Four Seasons in Dallas. Except for a fruitcake here and there, this tradition of the groom's cake is practically unheard of in the North, so I think we should consider it for our "something borrowed." There's something kind of sweet about giving the guy his due.

Now about that something blue . . .

## *The Best Man, or Who's Your Daddy?*

Yankees tend to go with blood brothers, frat brothers, brothers-in-law-to-be, and best friends. In the South, don't be surprised to see Daddy! Wardrobe doesn't vary all that much region to region, with one notable exception: Southern formal shops have powder blue tuxes in stock.

## *Cakes and Fakes*

Couples can save money by ordering enough to feed only half of their guests (a safe bet, according to wedding planners), but Southerners frown on the cost-cutting shortcut of iced cardboard (cake as prop), and resort to that only if absolutely necessary.

Although regional flavor always come into play, the Southern wedding cake is more likely to be traditional white iced than divine key lime, I'm afraid. Wedding cakes made out of stacks of "original glazed" are a rare if welcome sight. (Investors in Krispy Kreme need not worry: Cartons of Krispy Kremes have been working overtime as wedding favors.)

## *Stags and Shags*

### Still Single? Have a Double.

Yankee newlyweds and Southerner newlyweds have at least one thing in common. They can't be completely happy unless all of their single friends are married, too. Joyous brides and giddy grooms insist on cooking up ways to single out singles for attention.

### The Cake Pull
### (a Southern treat—especially popular in New Orleans)

Before the cake is cut, the bride invites all of the single women at the reception to sit at the cake table. The wedding cake has been baked with tiny silver charms inside the bottom layer. A white ribbon is attached to each charm, and the charms all carry a different forecast. The women each choose a ribbon, and, on the count of three, they pull the charm out to find out what their future will hold.

### The Shag

Beach music is all the rage at many Southern weddings (especially in the Carolinas), and couples shag the night away. With all due respect to Austin Powers, he misled us. Ask any Southerner. The shag is a dance.

Think jitterbug meets rhythm and blues meets sand. The basic shag is a 6-count swing dance with lots of fancy footwork danced to the likes of The Embers, Chairmen of the Board, and The Drifters. Originating on the shores of Myrtle Beach, the shag is still evolving. You can have your partner start out slowly with "the basic," and then advance to the fancier steps: the belly roll, boogie walk, duck walk, pivot, kickback with lean, prissy, applejack, and sugar foot.

**Yankee Do! If you want to dance in the South, you have to learn how to shag.**

**Yankee Don't! Do not do the chicken dance at a Southern wedding.**

### *The Gifts: Well-to-Do and Well, Don't!*

Traditionalists for the most part, Southern brides still love their silver, china, and crystal. Couples register their patterns and count on the church ladies to deliver the place settings in full, twelve-deep minimum. And they're rarely disappointed. Southern wedding guests know that it's *unrefined* to deviate from the bridal registry when buying wedding gifts. And nothing gives a Southern woman more pleasure than tracking down a discontinued heirloom silver pattern by calling on her Atlanta connections. (Unless, of course, it's using her coupon cards, opening a charge account to save 10 percent, and carrying the gift with her to save on shipping charges.)

**Yankee Don't! The practical gifts on the registry (towels, linens, etc.) are for the round-the-clock showers. Don't be "tacky" and give them as wedding presents. And giving money to a Southerner for a wedding gift is the ultimate faux pas!**

### The Gift Table

Displaying the loot is a tradition you can find on both sides of the Mason-Dixon Line, but it's the Southerners who really make an art out of it. A family member or friend of the bride will go through all of the gifts received before the wedding and spend an entire afternoon setting them up for the big presentation. She'll set a table with a mock formal setting, a mock everyday setting, and find just the right home for everything in between. It's customary in the South to see a coffeemaker, an enameled pot for butter beans, and a retro toaster flanked by the sterling silver iced tea spoons and the formal place setting. The gifts sit at their own table at the reception and get as many oohs and ahhs as the bride.

**Yankee Do! Send your wedding present early if you want it to have a seat at the table!**

## *The Bridal Portrait*

Southerners don't have their pictures taken. They have them "made." The bridal portrait is *made* before the wedding so the re-touched brides can get around. The bridal portrait is "must see," so it must be:

- Camera-ready for a prestigious newspaper bridal announcement
- Framed and hung in the bride's new home so for years and years she can think: What *was* I thinking with that hair?
- At her wedding reception so the guests can think: What *is* she thinking with that hair?
- Framed and hung in her parents' home so they can look at it and think: We got her married off. We can rest now.

## *North versus South: May the Best Man Win!*

| **You Know It's a Yankee Wedding When . . .** | **You Know It's a Southern Wedding When . . .** |
|---|---|
| The bride is pregnant. | The bride is barefoot. |
| There's a cash bar. | There's no bar. |
| The guests throw rice at the bride and groom. | The guests throw grits at the bride and groom. |
| The father of the bride sucker-punches the best man after his toast. | The father of the groom is the best man and skips the toast—he's Baptist. |
| A fistfight breaks out. | A catfight breaks out. |
| When they play Guns N' Roses. | When they shoot guns and wear roses. |
| The DJ stops the music to announce the winning Powerball numbers. | The preacher stops the sermon to announce a NASCAR pileup. |
| The bride and groom are women, and the ceremony is officiated by Elvis Costello. | The bride and groom are related, and the ceremony is officiated by Elvis Presley. |
| The maid of honor is a guy in drag. | The best man carries the rebel flag. |
| The mother of the bride walks down the aisle with a shot glass. | The father of the bride walks down the aisle with a shotgun. |
| The mother-son dance is "Sunrise, Sunset" from *Fiddler on the Roof.* | The mother-son dance is "You Ain't Woman Enough to Take My Man" by Loretta Lynn. |

| **You Know It's a Yankee Wedding When . . .** | **You Know It's a Southern Wedding When . . .** |
| --- | --- |
| The DJ mispronounces the couple's name in his boisterous rendition of "For the first time in public . . ." and someone throws a roll at him | The trendsetting couple hires a DJ to announce the wedding party and someone throws a biscuit at him. |
| Somebody is caught writing a check out at the dinner table when the bride and her purse arrive. ("Wanted to see what they were serving before I decided what to give.") | Somebody is caught tipping a flask when the bride and groom move past. |
| Somebody breaks something dancing (ankle, back, thumb, etc.). | Somebody shoots something prancing (five-prong, hop-a-long, Billy Bob, etc.). |
| There is a two-hour pause between the wedding and the reception. | The two-hour pause *is* the reception. |

**May we all live happily ever after.**

★ ★ ★ ★ ★ ★ ★ ★ ★

Chapter 10

★ ★ ★ ★ ★ ★ ★ ★ ★

# Moving South: The Twelve-Step Program

***Does it feel strange to live*** in a city where nobody knows your name? Does it seem as if it will be a lifetime before you'll see those old familiar faces? Will you ever feel like yourself again? Will you ever fit in? While I may not qualify as an expert in the field of relocation, I do offer five years of firsthand experience. Five years?! Has it been that long?! If I had killed my husband when he first dragged me down here, I could be up for parole by now. Still, I've taken it upon myself to put together some survival tips for Yankees at large. My twelve steps won't work for everybody, of course. They're more for beginners. And slow starters. Y'all got a problem with that?

## The Twelve Steps

1. Seek shelter in comfort foods. Pack on those pounds. (Remember, nobody knows what you used to look like.) Reacquaint yourself with fast food. The South has plenty of comfort foods to offer. (Personally, I prefer peach cobbler to grits.) Just tell your honey the scale got lost in the move.

2. Get rid of your accent. (Boston, Brooklyn, Jersey—it all sounds the same to Southerners.) Rent the film *Divine Secrets of the Ya-Ya Sisterhood,* and practice faking with the best of them.

3. Don't forget your cocktail shaker. But remember, no drinking before noon.

4. Have a garage sale the week you arrive. Place everything that got damaged in the move on the "antiques" table, and speak in a haughty tone, using terms like "vintage" and "distressed" when discussing price. Feel free to embellish each item with a little narrative, but you'll want to stay away from "This dates back to the Civil War."

5. When the Confederate flag comes up for discussion, offer to make the mint juleps.

6. Practice saying *"Ah like evruhbody; Ah like evruhthang."* Frontal lobotomies could be a big plus here. When you call the doctor for your lobotomy appointment, don't say "new patient." Your Southern accent is key here.

7. When you're tempted to say "This is how we did it up North," consider the ramifications—total isolation and your mug plastered on the post office most-wanted list.

8. Tradition is really big here, so bring along as many "SECRET FAMILY RECIPES" as you can steal from the Pillsbury Bake-Off files. Hand-write them on cards (stain your fingers with vanilla extract), and plant them right next to your *Joy of Cooking.* It's only illegal if you try to sell them.

9. In your best Southern drawl, say: "*Mah word, wherevuh are mah mannuz*?" instead of "ARE YOU TAWKIN' TO ME?" when the police pull you over for reckless driving (passing a Southern driver who doesn't know how to use a turn signal).

10. Confront. Confront. Confront. "Honey, I don't care about your stinkin' promotion; I want to go home." (If you didn't move here for a promotion, and your spouse looks at you confused, you can always say "See, this place is making me nuts.")

11. Learn to golf. Then the "weapons" in the golf bag won't get you in trouble when Mr. or Ms. Promotion (the one who moved you away from career, family, and friends) is found at the bottom of the lake. You can tell the officers you were "jus' practicin' mah swing." If the lady's golf club does not fit, they must acquit.

12. On the next sunny day, stand under the longleaf pines, look up at the "Carolina blue" sky, throw your Southern belle hat up in the air Mary Tyler Moore–style, and sing in your worst Nanny inflection, "I'm going to make it after aw."

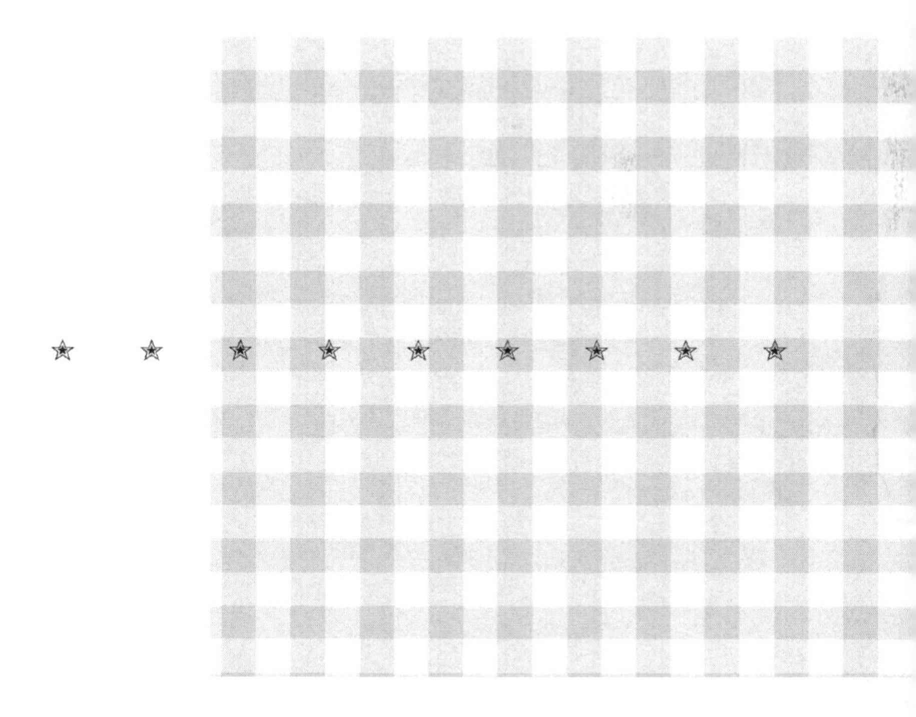

## *And If That Doesn't Work*

The best advice I can give any Yankee moving South is to adapt at your own pace, on your own terms. Don't expect success overnight—from the South or from yourself. The South seems to want to meet you halfway, but from what I can tell, you have to give first. That doesn't mean you have to say good-bye to the person formerly known as you. You may never develop a Southern accent and may always prefer a Philly cheesesteak to biscuits and gravy, but you're ahead of the game just for knowing the difference. A bigger world is a better world. Instead of only caring about all things North or all things West, you'll care about all, okay, most things South, too. Like hurricanes, Southern politicians, college ball, and the soldiers from Fort Bragg or the base nearest you, just to name a few.

Moving is hard. Pretending it isn't is harder. But now that I know making a move is good for you, I can't recommend it highly enough. It's such fertile ground for personal growth. Finding out that "home" is a portable concept is a wondrous thing. Having to reinvent yourself and transition your family into the unknown can be an overwhelming upheaval, but it also can be packed full of opportunities and fun surprises.

Don't think of it as a lifelong move, but rather a long vacation. You know how it's the unexplored territory that makes a vacation fun? And you see the natives for what's good about them, not what's wrong with them? It would help to face a move like that, too. Instead of panicking when it seems so different, see it as an adventure. And the next thing you know, the move no longer defines you, and your vacation has lasted five years and counting.

You learn a lot about yourself when you move. I was entirely unprepared for how bad I would feel when I first got here and even less prepared for how great I feel now. It's true what they say: Disappointment equals unrealistic expectations. So I just wanted to let you know what to expect.

## *I Wish Someone Had Told Me . . .*

- Many of the people who are saying "You're not from around here, are ya?" are not Southerners trying to make you feel out of place. They're Yankees trying to sniff out their own. Bite back. Ask where they're from.
- There's a statute of limitations on Southern hospitality. Southerners lay it on thick for Yankee tourists, not Yankee transplants. Tell 'em you're here to stay, and you'll be taking that peach cobbler "to go."
- Why it's so much cheaper to rent a beach house in August. It's not the heat *or* the humidity: It's the hurricanes.
- Hurricane preparedness does not mean a manicure, a pedicure, and a copy of *The New Yorker.*
- I'd talk to my mom, my best friends, and my nephew Tommy more often, not less often, since moving to Raleigh.
- It takes *at least* a year to adjust to a move.
- Down here, the customer is always right . . . right of Jesse Helms.
- That the moving company will never find the big box labeled "second floor blue bedroom." No worries. Guest bedrooms seem way bigger without the bed.
- You're not being unreasonable. You *can* get a better haircut in Philadelphia. That's why the airlines created weekend discount fares!

Southerners will tell you it's the hospitality that makes it so great down here. But if you ask me, you learn more from the outsiders. Here's what some transplants from Philadelphia, New York, Kenya, Chicago, Michigan, Mexico, South Dakota, Boston, Seattle, Arizona, Ireland, Minnesota, India, Rhode Island, Connecticut, Cleveland, France, and New Jersey had to say.

## 100 Southern Things Worth the Trip

**1.** crepe myrtles **2**. hush puppies **3.** longleaf pines **4.** driving the Blue Ridge Parkway in the fall **5.** Emerald Isle, NC, beaches **6.** St. Patrick's Day in Savannah **7**. The Grove Park Inn **8**. mild winters **9.** early summers **10.** late falls **11**. crawfish boils in Louisiana **12.** Pinehurst No. 2 **13.** Bloody Marys at the Pinehurst Hotel **14.** going to sleep to the sound of cicadas **15.** hiking up Chimney Rock Park, NC **16**. coffee and beignets in New Orleans **17.** brunch at Commander's Palace **18.** the French Quarter **19.** Beale Street in Memphis **20.** Sanibel Island **21.** "Ding" Darling **22.** the Kentucky Derby **23.** the Great Smokey Mountains **24.** the Mall in Washington, DC **25.** cherry blossoms **26.** The Greenbrier in West Virginia **27.** dinner at Magnolia Grill **28.** South of the Border **29.** antebellum mansions **30.** the Duke Chapel, especially the view driving up **31**. an ACC home game **32.** Maryland crabs **33.** Dreamland Barbecue in Tuscaloosa, AL **34.** Charleston—don't miss St. Patty's Day **35.** snorkeling in Key West **36.** sliced BBQ at Bullock's in Durham **37.** Durham Bulls game, where you need to chant, "gimme a D-E-R-M, what's the spell? Durham!" **38.** Graceland and buying Love Me Tender shampoo at the gift shop **39.** fishin' in the Eno around the Rhododendron Bluffs **40.** the Outer Banks **41.** illegal dance clubs **42.** Seaside, FL **43.** Jimmy Buffett and all things Parrothead **44.** living the classics: "I learned to speak English reading *Tom Sawyer,* and it happened right here!" **45.** the National Museum of Naval Aviation in Pensacola **46.** Bellingrath Gardens in Alabama **47.** the New Orleans Aquarium **48.** the Naval Academy in Annapolis **49**. people-watching in South Beach **50.** Oakwood Cemetery in Raleigh, NC **51.** the vegetation, the greens **52.** Pawley's Island, SC **53.** the Intracoastal Waterway between Jacksonville, FL, and Charleston, SC **54.** Jack Daniel's whisky distillery in Lynchburg, TN **55.** Gatlinburg and Pigeon Forge, TN, in the Smokey Mountains on the Appalachian Trail **56.** Dollywood, Dolly Parton's Smokey Mountain theme park in Pigeon Forge, TN **57.** the grand homes in Savannah **58.** magnolias and dogwoods **59.** the ducks on parade in the lobby of the Peabody Hotel in Memphis **60.** moonshine **61.** fried green tomatoes **62.** the Grand Ole Opry **63.** Disney World **64.** the Everglades **65.** St. Augustine Alligator Farm Zoological Park **66.** 'Bama home games **67.** the River Walk in San Antonio **68.** the seashells in St. Augustine, FL **69.** riding the bull at Gilly's **70.** sailing in Oriental, NC **71.** Sullivan's Steak House in North Dallas **72.** Kentucky Bourbon Trail **73.** Louisville Slugger Museum **74.** Camden Yards **75.** Sea World **76.** amateur night at the Down Home Pickin' Parlor in Johnson City, TN (guitar pickers and banjo players come down out of the mountains of Tennessee and North Carolina) **77.** watching a space shuttle launch at Cape Canaveral **78.** Las Olas Boulevard in Fort Lauderdale **79.** vinegar-style barbecue **80.** tailgating at NASCAR **81.** leaves changing in Asheville **82.** less stress than the big cities, "like a siesta, a long nap" **83.** swimming with the manatees in Crystal River, FL **84.** biking on Bald Head Island, NC **85.** Junior League yard sales **86.** year-round golf **87.** camping in the Appalachian Mountains **88.** shagging **89.** shopping in Coconut Grove, FL **90.** Colonial Williamsburg **91.** the women **92.** mountain music **93.** shrimp and grits in Charleston **94.** deep-fried turkeys for Thanksgiving **95.** the accents **96.** whitewater rafting on the Nantahala River **97.** Cape Hatteras Lighthouse **98.** Provision Seafood Company **99.** pig pickin's **100.** Carolina blue skies

***What can I say?*** It just sneaks up on you. And all of a sudden, you're home. And here's the best part. When I take the Raleigh-to-Philly flight, no matter which way the plane is headed, I'm always coming home.

## Acknowledgments

To Trish Todd at Simon & Schuster, for taking my not-ready-for-primetime idea and making it so much better: If it weren't for your vision for this book and your spot-on line edit, I wouldn't be here. And neither would the readers. I was lucky enough to find myself in the hands of one of New York's top editors-in-chief who also happened to be a Southern belle from Tennessee. Serendipity? Maybe. But I think it was my agent, Rob Wilson.

Rob, one of my biggest highs was the day you agreed to represent me. You sold my book in a month—and you thought that was long. I think that says it all. That, and you played for the New York Yankees. (Not relevant, but oh so cool!)

To my parents, Marie Ryan Duffin and Jack Duffin, and Michael's mom, Eileen Schuett Ward: If they're cloning role models, they need look no further. (Don't miss my mom in the latest Cameron Diaz movie!)

To my extraordinary brothers and sister, John, Tom, Denise, and Brian: Coming from a big family is truly life's greatest gift. Thanks for your insight, your friendship, your wives (Janice and Noreen) and your kids!

To my nephews and nieces, who know I'm crazy about them: Tommy! Duffin, Sean, Katie, Allie, and Brianna, and all of the wonderful Wards.

Word may have Spellcheck, but only a true friend can do Funnycheck. Thanks to Barbara Brandfass, Jan Lawrence, Mary Ann Miller, Rosina Rucci, Kathy Ruyak, and my cousin Connie Cichon Watko for adding laughs in all the right places. (The good sport award goes to my sister-in-law Sue Ward who gave me the okay to use her family's name in vain.) And to the rest of my friends who may not have helped with this book but helped with my life, I thank you enormously! Special mention to Deira Gerritsen for the lifeline from Boston my first year in Raleigh.

Finally, huge thanks to Thad Ogburn for my first newspaper column; Jerry Agar for launching our *Don't You Be My Neighbor* radio show; Phil Dickerson, a.k.a. Native Son, for your Southern expertise, and Joanne Cini, for your author's expertise. To the readers of my column and listeners to our radio show, to all of the people who've ever moved (especially the ones who helped with my 100 Southern Things Worth the Trip list), this one's for you.

20766992R00103

Made in the USA
Middletown, DE
07 June 2015